ESTRENO Collection of Contemporary Spanish Plays

General Editor: Phyllis Zatlin

PARTING GESTURES

with

A NIGHT IN THE SUBWAY

PALOMA PEDRERO

PARTING GESTURES

(El color de agosto
La noche dividida,
Resguardo personal)

with

A NIGHT IN THE SUBWAY

(Solos esta noche)

Translated by Phyllis Zatlin

ESTRENO Plays
New Brunswick, New Jersey
1999

ESTRENO Contemporary Spanish Plays 6
General Editor: Phyllis Zatlin
Department of Spanish & Portuguese-FAS
105 George Street., New Brunswick, New Jersey
Rutgers, The State University of New Jersey 08901-1414 USA

Library of Congress Cataloging in Publication Data
Pedrero, Paloma, 1957-
Parting Gestures and A Night in the Subway
Bibliography:
Contents: The Color of August. A Night Divided. The Voucher. A Night in the Subway.
Translations of: El color de agosto. La noche dividida. Resguardo personal. Solos esta noche.
1. Pedrero, Paloma, 1957- Translations, English.
I. Zatlin, Phyllis. II. Title.
Library of Congress Catalog Card No.: 98-073219
ISBN: 1-888463-06-6

Revised Edition

The original edition of this volume was prepared and published with the support of the Dirección General del Libro y Bibliotecas of the Ministerio de Cultura de España and of the Program for Cultural Cooperation between Spain's Ministry of Culture and United States' Universities.

Cover: Jeffrey Eads

TABLE OF CONTENTS

A NOTE ON *PARTING GESTURES*

These works by Paloma Pedrero offer three artfully crafted character studies which illuminate some of the oldest and most familiar traits in human relationships (the struggle for power and control, the depths of cruelty, and the paradox of loving and hating at the same time) in fiercely modern situations and language. Together, the plays make a visually rich and emotionally compelling evening of theatre that will give audiences food for thought as well as for feelings.

The Voucher is a quick sketch which establishes the playwright's major themes. A couple's willingness to sacrifice their beloved dog in order to torture each other draws, in broad strokes, the cruelty which is in all three works. The ending shakes up the audience's assumptions about the power relationship. *A Night Divided* adds depth and shading to the themes introduced in *The Voucher*. It explores the many ways in which the characters are divided from each other despite their efforts to connect, and connected despite their desires to be free, building to a bittersweet and ironic ending. *The Color of August* is the painting which fully develops and colors the picture outlined in *The Voucher* and *A Night Divided.* The complex relationship is played out through a series of evocative and erotic physical and verbal exchanges. In one moment, the women literally paint their frustration, anger, and desire onto each other's bodies, a dramatic combination of spontaneous action and ritual imagery.

Pedrero's characters show many of the familiar faces of lovers everywhere--the controller, the controlled, the deceiver and the deceived. Phyllis Zatlin's translation captures the studiedly natural speech patterns of the liar, the plotter, and the lover; the plays' comfortable English diction retains a distinctly Spanish feel.

The collection provides an attractive range of characters and situations for the actor; the small cast size (two men and two women) puts it within the range of almost any producer. Paloma Pedrero's plays invite exploration by American theatres and audiences.

Janet Finegar
Literary Manager
The Wilma Theater (Philadelphia)

AN ADDITIONAL NOTE ON *A NIGHT IN THE SUBWAY*

Paloma Pedrero's plays are a pleasure to stage. For actors, they offer situations with the opportunity to engage in highly imaginative, theatrical "stuff." An artist and her estranged artist-model get naked and paint each other madly in the middle of *The Color of August*. A Bible salesman walks into a house only to be asked by the lady of the house to stab her in *A Night Divided*. Trapped on a dark subway platform, a woman spontaneously offers up all of her valuables to a stranger in *A Night in the Subway*. Each play is loaded with action, and often with humor.

While humor plays a big role, these are not merely light romantic comedies. There are unexpected, subtle nuances which fill each character with dimension. The characters are honest. Masking and unmasking is widespread in Pedrero's plays. There is a constant interplay between the character's mask and the character's humanity. Something is hidden in each of Pedrero's central figures. Something is masked, something is not just what it seems to be. Carmen in *A Night in the Subway* is not just a comic, bourgeois bureaucrat. That is only a mask for the frustrated, passionate woman inside, who is willing to become intimate and unmask herself. Pedrero plays with our (and her characters') perceptions, dangling out images and contrasting them with inner truths and actualities.

It is no surprise that Pedrero is an excellent actress. Her writer's sensibility is distinctly, viscerally, theatrical. She knows what a play needs to make it entertaining and playable. This certainly showed in her delightful American performance of *A Night in the Subway* in 1997 and is also clear in all of her plays. Not for her the realm of stuffy closet literary dramas or strained thesis plays.

But this is not to say that Pedrero's theatre is lacking in ideas. There is so much for a director to explore, particularly with such issues as gender and identity. In these romances and conflicts between women and men, you are drawn to question and view what exactly gender means, how much is socially constructed, how much is inherent, in a refreshing new light.

If you are looking for exciting works to stage, look no further. These plays are immediate, alive, tangible. They provide enjoyable challenges to actor, director and audience alike. I heartily recommend them as viable pieces of theatre.

Christopher Mack
Director, New York City

PALOMA PEDRERO

Paloma Pedrero, one of contemporary Spain's most important and innovative women playwrights, was born in Madrid in 1957. An actress, director, and theatre teacher, as well as a prize-winning author, she is associated with an independent theatre movement that wishes to explore, in realistic language, topics of concern to a younger generation of spectators. Her full-length and one-act plays are being staged with increasing frequency in Spain, Latin America, the United States, Great Britain, France and other European countries.

Pedrero's earliest drama, *La llamada de Lauren* (*Lauren's Call*), premiered in Spain in 1985. Typical of several of her works, it is a two-character play that reveals a moment of crisis in a relationship and a search for identity. In this case, a couple on their third wedding anniversary confront the problems with their marriage when the husband's cross-dressing as Lauren Bacall for carnival uncovers his basic dissatisfaction with the macho role assigned him by society. Pedrero's most performed play to date is the one included in this volume: *El color de agosto* (*The Color of August*). Like *Lauren's Call*, it develops a moment of great dramatic intensity in the relationship between its two characters.

Her other full-length works include *Invierno de luna alegre* (*The Winter of the Happy Moon*), winner of the 1987 Tirso de Molina prize, and *Besos de lobos* (*Wolf Kisses*), which received its world premiere in 1991 at Hobart and William Smith Colleges in the United States. Each of these two texts has five characters, who may be viewed as archetypes, and action that extends over a period of time. *La isla amarilla* (*The Yellow Island*), a fanciful satire of Western "civilization" from the perspective of "primitive" Samoans, has been staged to acclaim in various theatres in the Madrid area by a unique acting group from a women's prison. *Locas de amar* (*Love Crazy*), a satire of what happens when a middle-aged wife is dumped by a husband in pursuit of younger women, was directed by the author at Madrid's municipal Centro Cultural de la Villa in 1996. *Una estrella* (*First Star*), a psychodrama of a woman seeking to understand her dead father, a drunkard and gambler who had neglected his wife and children, was performed in France, Spain, and the United States in 1998.

The trilogy of one-act plays, *Noches de amor efímero* (*Nights of Passing Love*), was first staged in 1990, and has been translated to English and French. The underlying unity of these two-character works is provided by a common focus on an intense but fleeting moment of intimacy. Pedrero continues to write short works, adding to the *Nights'* collection and exploring other subjects as well.

Pedrero's theatre in general is characterized by its overt metatheatricalism, her constant questioning of traditional social norms, particularly sex roles; and her skill at synthesizing dramatic elements, thus creating plays that may be staged with relatively small casts and limited sets.

Inquiries regarding permissions should be addressed to the author through the

D. Alfredo Carrión Saiz
Director de Artes Escénicas
Sociedad General de Autores y Editores
Fernando VI, 4
28004 Madrid
Spain
Phone: 34-91-349 96 86 Fax: 34-91-349-97-12

or through the translator:

Prof. Phyllis Zatlin
Department of Spanish & Portuguese-FAS
Rutgers, The State University
105 George Street, New Brunswick, NJ 08901-1414
Phone: 1-732-932-9412x25
Fax: 1-732-932-9837
Email: zatlin@rci.rutgers.edu

El color de agosto was first staged in July 1988 at the Centro Cultural Galileo in Madrid under the direction of Pepe Ortega. It had its American university premiere 5-8 December 1991 at the Pace Downtown Theater at Schimmel Center for the Arts, New York City, under the direction of Timur Djordjadze. It was given professional staged readings in London by the Loose Change Theatre Company 5 and 7 March 1992, under the direction of Tessa Schneideman, and at Applause Books in New York City, 9 June 1998, under the direction of Christopher Mack.

La noche dividida was first staged in November 1990 by the Teatro del Beso Company, under the direction of Jesús Cracio, at the Alfil Theatre in Madrid. It had its American university premiere 5-8 December 1991 at the Pace Downtown Theater at Schimmel Center for the Arts, New York City, under the direction of Timur Djordjadze. It was given a professional staged reading 29 March 1997 in London at the West Yorkshire Playhouse, Leeds, under the direction of Roxana Silbert and produced at the Penn State Pavilion Theatre, 20 September 1997, under the direction of Mark Fearnow.

Resguardo personal was first staged in 1986 at an authors' workshop of the Centro Nacional de Nuevas Tendencias Escénicas in Madrid, under the direction of Paloma Pedrero. *The Voucher* had its American university premiere 5-8 December 1991 at the Pace Downtown Theater at Schimmel Center for the Arts, New York City, under the direction of Timur Djordjadze. It was given a professional staged reading 29 March 1997 in London at the West Yorkshire Playhouse, Leeds, under the direction of Roxana Silbert. Staged readings by drama students were given in September 1997 at Loyola University (New Orleans), Ohio Wesleyan College, Colgate University and Union College. *The Voucher* was first published in *The Literary Review*, Volume 36, Number 3 (Spring 1993) in a special issue devoted to the literature of democratic Spain (1975-1992), edited by Cecilia C. Lee.

Solos esta noche was first staged in November 1990 by the Teatro del Beso Company, under the direction of Jesús Cracio, at the Alfil Theatre in Madrid. It had its American university premiere 9-10 December 1997 in New Orleans at the Lower Depths Theater (Loyola University), under the direction of Paola Ruiz de Pellón. It was published in *Collages & Bricolages* 7 (1993; Alternate Title: *Tonight We're Alone*).

Désirée Ortega and Charo Sabio in a 1990 staging
of *El color de agosto* by
ALBANTA ACCION in Cádiz.
Directed by Charlie Keaton.

THE COLOR OF AUGUST

CHARACTERS

Maria Dehesa
Laura Anton

A brightly lit artist's studio, with lots of windows. Paintings and panels on the walls. Easels, sculptures. This is a somewhat disorganized but luxurious space with a certain air of affectation.

Center stage there is a fountain-shower with a little angel that spouts water from its mouth to another angel hanging above it with its mouth open. (By moving the bottom angel, the upper one begins to spout water, thus converting into a sophisticated shower.)

A refrigerator, a television set, a fan. Also at center stage, a plaster of Paris Venus with a bird cage in her abdomen; there is a live bird in the cage.

It is early evening on a hot August day.

MARIA enters from the garden. She is a young-looking thirty-five. She is wearing a long, sleeveless T-shirt like a mini-skirt, thus revealing her long, tanned legs. Her hair is cut in the latest style with uneven, colored shocks. MARIA matches her studio perfectly. She is carrying flowers that she arranges in a large vase. She turns on the television and plugs in the fan. She puts on music. She goes over to the answering machine and plays it. Among all the other sounds, we can hear a man's voice on the machine. MARIA arranges things in the studio without seeming to notice the noise.)

MARIA (*Both nervous and happy, she goes over to the cage and plays with the bird*): That's it. That's it. Sing, go ahead, sing. (*She picks up a portfolio and takes out several canvases that she begins hanging on the wall. They are all drawings and sketches of the same woman. In some we see Maria alongside the other woman. As she hangs them, she recites their titles:*) Laura with an apple. Laura with the Big Dipper. A sad Laura. Laura sitting. Laura with a garbage can.

An old Laura. Laura looking at Maria . . . (*She looks uneasily at her watch.*) Eight o'clock! (*She paces nervously. She sits down in front of the television. She jumps up and decides to paint. She is worried and cannot concentrate. Suddenly, seized by an idea, she turns off all the machines and covers the cage with a black cloth. The room becomes silent. The only noise is that of the water in the fountain. After a few moments, the doorbell rings. MARIA runs and takes the cover off of the bird.*) Sing, come on, sing! (*She gets ready to open the door. She takes a deep breath. She crosses to the door, opens it slightly, and quickly hides.*)

LAURA'S VOICE (*From offstage*): Hello? May I come in? (*LAURA slowly enters the studio. Although we can guess that she is the woman in the paintings, she has changed radically. She is older and less attractive. Her clothes are inexpensive, and she has not taken care of her skin. Her eyes, perhaps, are more beautiful, more alive, more genuine than those in the pictures. LAURA looks around at the studio and, upon seeing her portraits, freezes. After a long pause, she reacts. Frightened, she glances around her, looking for someone. Almost involuntarily, she crosses to the outside door. MARIA enters.*)

MARIA: Laura!

(*For a moment, they look at each other in silence. MARIA runs over to Laura, closes the door, and hugs her.*)

MARIA: Why didn't you tell me you'd come back? You're . . . you're . . . (*She steps back and looks at Laura.*) You . . . you look great. A little thin maybe. So? Aren't you going to say anything? Aren't you glad to see me?

LAURA: Yes.

MARIA: Well come on, come on in. Make yourself comfortable. You're sweating.

LAURA: It's very hot out.

MARIA: Cool yourself off in the fountain. Come on . . .

LAURA: Never mind. Forget it.

MARIA: I'll go put on the fan.

LAURA: Don't bother on my account.

MARIA: Come sit down. (*LAURA does not sit down.*) Tell me. How'd you like the surprise?

LAURA (*Pulling herself together*): A bit sudden.

MARIA (*Taking Laura's hands*): Why are you trembling?

LAURA (*Pulling away*): I'm not trembling.

MARIA (*Hugging her*): I'm so happy. I can hardly believe it. Come on, sit down here. What would you like to drink?

LAURA: It doesn't matter.

MARIA: Whiskey. I've got a special bottle just for you. Would you like some?

(*LAURA nods her head. MARIA takes out the bottle and prepares the glasses. LAURA looks around the studio.*) Do you like it?
LAURA: Oh yes. Very much.
MARIA: Yeah, but all of us don't fit anymore.
LAURA: All of you?
MARIA: Besides the bird, I've got two cats in the garden.
LAURA: Cats? In the garden?
MARIA: Yes. I have a garden out back.
LAURA: But you never liked cats. Every time I brought one home, you kicked it out.
MARIA (*Handing her a glass*): I learned to understand them. I decided to learn, and I did. (*In a lighthearted tone.*) Besides, in a garden you can have cats--and in an attic you can't. (*She raises her glass.*) Say something.
LAURA: To your success.
MARIA: To our reunion.

(*They drink.*)

LAURA: Why . . . why did you make me come here?
MARIA: I went to an agency looking for a model and I saw your picture. I almost died. Why didn't you call me to say you'd returned?
LAURA: I haven't returned yet.
MARIA: So I thought I'd give you a surprise and I gave the woman at the agency a fake name. (*She laughs.*) Of course she recognized me right off, and real surprised, she said, "But you're Maria Dehesa." And I, with a straight face, I said, "I wish I were! No, I'm . . . "
LAURA (*Throwing at her the piece of paper that she has been holding in her hand*): Carmen Robles.
MARIA: That's right. I was so surprised to see your picture that I couldn't wait to see you. But tell me. When did you get here from New York? How did things go there? Why did you stop writing me? Why are you working as a model?
LAURA: Which question do you want me to answer first?
MARIA (*Rapping herself on the forehead*): Stupid! How stupid of me! We've spent our whole lives together and I still haven't learned that you hate interrogations.
LAURA: Our whole lives--except eight years.
MARIA: True. Eight years is a long time, isn't it?
LAURA: Yes.
MARIA: But you haven't changed.
LAURA: Don't lie. I've changed. So have you. A lot. You seem taller. (*MARIA laughs.*) You must have stretched.
MARIA (*After a pause*): How are you?
LAURA: Wonderful. Can't you tell?

MARIA: I . . . I . . .
LAURA (*Getting up*): How would you like me to pose? With clothes or nude?
MARIA: Don't be ridiculous. That was just an excuse. Just an excuse to see you.
LAURA: And did you ask yourself if I wanted to see you?
MARIA: Well . . .
LAURA: They hired me for two hours. Tell me where you want me.
MARIA: Don't be silly. We have so many things to tell each other.
LAURA: Really? I think we already know enough about one another. I've seen you in art galleries and magazines. I know about your prizes and your studio. I've come to work.
MARIA: I don't know anything about you.
LAURA: Oh, really? Haven't you been able to find out? Well, as you see, I pose for a hobby. You guessed that, right?
MARIA: Listen, I wanted . . .
LAURA: Well, are you going to paint me or not?
MARIA: I . . . I'll pay you anyway.
LAURA (*After a pause*): Thanks but I want more than that. Just for you I come more expensive.
MARIA: How much?
LAURA: How much are you offering?
MARIA: Whatever you want.
LAURA (*Pointing to a painting*): That.
MARIA: Do you like it?
LAURA: How much is it worth?
MARIA: For you?
LAURA: On the market.
MARIA: Five thousand.
LAURA: I want two of those.
MARIA: I don't have two.
LAURA: One's not very much.
MARIA: If you pose for me, I'll give you as many as you like.
LAURA: Three.
MARIA (*After a moment*): All right.
LAURA: You need me that much? I would have thought with time . . .
MARIA: This is absurd! You know, I don't understand anything . . .
LAURA: You brought it on yourself. Well, no, dear, not for three or for eight, or for fifteen. I'm not going to pose for you. (*She heads toward the door.*)
MARIA: Where are you going?
LAURA: Away. Forget that you saw me. Okay? Someday I'll call you, "and if you like," we can see each other.
MARIA: No, please, don't go.

LAURA: This atmosphere is suffocating.
MARIA (*Pleading*): I spent all day getting ready to see you.
LAURA: To deceive me.
MARIA: I made your favorite dessert: the one with truffles and whipped cream.
LAURA: Thank you, Maria, but I don't like it anymore. (*She opens the door.*)
MARIA: Why?
LAURA: That's a dreadful montage.
MARIA (*Defeated*): Sure. Nothing moves. I thought I had everything clear. (*Beat.*) What an idiot I am! I had everything clear until I saw you.
LAURA: You did a fine job of disguising it. Congratulations. Goodbye.
MARIA: Don't be cruel.
LAURA: What do you want from me?
MARIA (*After a pause*): Nothing.

(*LAURA is about to leave. Suddenly she turns around. The two women look at each other a moment and embrace affectionately.*)

MARIA: Forgive me. Forgive me.
LAURA: Now I recognize you.
MARIA: My God, I thought you were leaving!
LAURA: Leave? When there are truffles and good whiskey?
MARIA: I hate you.
LAURA: I hate you.
MARIA: Let's have a drink.
LAURA: Yes, I could use one.

(*MARIA fills their glasses and they drink.*)

LAURA: I think we ought to start over.
MARIA: How?
LAURA: On equal terms. You've prepared it all so well. On your turf and armed to the teeth. I came unarmed.
MARIA: We're equal now. You disarmed me.
LAURA: You're silly. (*Beat.*) You really wanted to impress me, didn't you?
MARIA: It was an illusion I had. I forgot how strong you are.
LAURA: You look beautiful. You can see that life has treated you well.
MARIA: Yes.
LAURA: Say, what do you feel?
MARIA: When?
LAURA: When you reach success.

MARIA (*Thinking it through*): I don't know. You feel, you live. I have everything I ever wanted: this, a house with a swimming pool, two maids, a husband.
LAURA: Ah, so the husband's part of the success package?
MARIA: I didn't say that.
LAURA: Yes you did.
MARIA (*After a pause*): Maybe so. And you?
LAURA: And me what?
MARIA: You get married?
LAURA: Me? (*She laughs.*) No, dear. (*Beat.*) My God it's hot.
MARIA: Would you like some more?
LAURA: No thanks. Well, just a little more. I'm so thirsty.
MARIA: I have more bottles. Come on, make yourself comfortable. Take off your shoes. (*She takes them off for her.*) Tell me, how did things go?
LAURA: No.
MARIA: Why?
LAURA: I don't want to talk about the past.
MARIA: Just one question, okay?
LAURA: Just one.
MARIA: Did you forget him?
LAURA: Who? (*She gets up and looks at the paintings.*)
MARIA: Don't pretend you don't know. Juan.
LAURA (*With a nervous laugh*): Oh, yes. It was easy.
MARIA: Not so easy. You had to go off on a long trip.
LAURA (*Referring to one of the paintings*): It's surprising. In eight years you've completely changed your view of the world.
MARIA: Have we grown apart?
LAURA: That's a uterus?
MARIA: Yes.
LAURA: There's fire inside. And a fossil, some live thing. Maybe a snail that's looking for the way out.
MARIA: Yes.
LAURA: But the way out is covered over by an enormous monolith.
MARIA (*Anxiously*): Do you like it?
LAURA: That hand is dead.
MARIA: I was trying . . .
LAURA: Everything is anesthetized, perfect, motionless.
MARIA: You don't like it.
LAURA: It's nice.
MARIA: That's the latest one.
LAURA: Spring.
MARIA: Could be.

LAURA: A man/woman coming out of the water with fishes on his/her head.
MARIA: It's a woman.
LAURA: She has a penis.
MARIA: That's a fish.
LAURA: Why is she cross-eyed?
MARIA: She's not cross-eyed. She's looking up.
LAURA: That's what you think. It looks more like she's either going to have a stroke or an attack of indigestion.
MARIA: You don't like it.
LAURA: It's nice.
MARIA (*Showing her the easel with a blank canvas*): This is the latest one.
LAURA: That's the best one.
MARIA (*Pointing to the Venus*): That Venus with the bird in her abdomen and a hand opening the cage. A woman's hand.
LAURA (*Stepping behind the statue and putting her hand in the cage*): Like this?
MARIA: Let's see . . . A little lower.
LAURA: Like this?
MARIA: Wait. Give her a big hug. That's pretty! Your hand in the cage. That's it. No, don't move your fingers. (*LAURA moves them.*) The fingers tense. More. Let's see . . . (*She takes a pencil and begins to sketch. LAURA changes the composition.*) Don't move. Let me see it.
LAURA: No. Don't even imagine it. Don't even imagine it. (*She removes herself.*)
MARIA: It was beautiful.
LAURA: If I were you, I'd put in a plastic hand, or an iron hand. That's it, a pirate's hook.
MARIA: I'd like to see your things. I've missed them a lot. You were a great teacher for me.
LAURA (*Laughing*): A poor teacher. You didn't learn anything.
MARIA: People who know don't say that.
LAURA (*Touching Maria's hair*): Of course. It was a joke. (*She drinks.*)
MARIA: I sell a lot. I've been lucky. And you?
LAURA: Me, too.
MARIA: At what?
LAURA (*Screaming*): Aaugh!!
MARIA: What's wrong?
LAURA: I think we're going to have to start over. The truth or I leave.
MARIA: I don't understand you.
LAURA: We're faking.
MARIA: It's difficult to start after so many years.
LAURA (*Pouring herself a drink*): We'll have to drink.
MARIA: Yes. (*They drink.*)

LAURA: Go on, take a good look at me.
MARIA: I'm looking at you.
LAURA: And I'm looking at you. Come over here. (*She moves in front of a mirror, and MARIA follows her.*)
MARIA: You always had bigger tits than I did. The first time I saw you in the shower I thought: I'll never have tits like that.
LAURA: We were twelve years old. You were flat-chested.
MARIA: But I still never had them. So nice and round and with such clear nipples. I never had your face, or your hair, or your legs, or your hands, or your voice.
LAURA: You had your own. You couldn't have mine.
MARIA: I didn't have anything.
LAURA: Not anything?
MARIA: Never your talent.
LAURA: What's that?
MARIA: A light . . . It's like a birthmark. You come into the world with it clinging to your skin.
LAURA: And where is it hiding?
MARIA (*Tapping her on the head*): Here.
LAURA: No.
MARIA: Not in the tits.
LAURA: I don't know. I don't know. (*She drinks.*) You know something? I like this. You know something else? You're as nostalgic as a dead person. Yes, you're dead. Young, very young and pretty but . . . fame and money have made you too perfect. Incredibly perfect.
MARIA: You seem old.
LAURA: Does that make you happy?
MARIA (*Laughing*): Yes.
LAURA: But I'm alive. Look, look at me.
MARIA: And you're still bad.
LAURA: Still? And you still need me.
MARIA: Not now. I went on without you and I have everything. You, the great genius, Laura Anton, zap, down the tubes.
LAURA: And in spite of that, you still need me.
MARIA: No.
LAURA: Don't pretend. You wrote me more than a thousand letters. You made this appointment behind my back . . .
MARIA: I want to help you.
LAURA: Really?
MARIA: I know that you're living in poverty.
LAURA: Okay. I think we're dropping the act.
MARIA: I want to get you out of it.

LAURA: What a ridiculous little fountain.
MARIA: I want you to stop posing for other people.
LAURA (*Wetting herself*): It's so hot! (*She drinks.*)
MARIA: You're handicapped and you need me.
LAURA: You need me!
MARIA: I do? For what?
LAURA: You ought to know.
MARIA: I don't want you to pose for anyone else.
LAURA (*Laughing*): Look at the silly little girl . . .
MARIA: That's what I always was for you. A perfect idiot that you could use as a canvas or an old rag. But life switched roles on us. You always used me. You always buried me in garbage. I was a slave that you didn't even feed. And I couldn't begin to breathe until you went away. God, you don't know how grateful I was to Juan for leaving you!
LAURA: You're mistaken. He never left me because he never took me.
MARIA: That's true. Of the three of us, he was the smartest. Juan had . . .
LAURA: I don't want to talk about it!
MARIA: Why?
LAURA: It's been eight years. It's over. You understand?
MARIA: Didn't you say that he didn't matter to you?
LAURA: He doesn't matter to me!
MARIA: Don't you want to know anything about him?
LAURA: No.
MARIA: I know some things that . . .
LAURA: I'm not interested!
MARIA: I don't believe you. You tense up when I mention his name. Let's see. Juaann, Juaann . . .
LAURA: How you've sharpened your claws. That surprises me. I always thought you were . . .
MARIA: That I was a polecat.
LAURA (*Laughing*): That you were a bit of a polecat, right?
MARIA: But now I have long claws. (*She scratches Laura.*)
LAURA: You've hurt me.
MARIA: So have you.
LAURA: What do you want from me?
MARIA: I've got a lot of gold. I want to give it to you.
LAURA: So you've run out of ideas? (*She drinks.*)
MARIA: You're drunk.
LAURA: So what?
MARIA: I want to salvage a genius for humanity.
LAURA (*She cracks up laughing*): How stupid! Don't you have a better argument?

MARIA: I love you.

LAURA (*After a pause*): And you have a lot of money.

MARIA: Yes. (*LAURA begins to cry.*) Laura, Laurie, forgive me. I'm such a bitch, I know but . . . You are the best . . . You can't be like that . . . like that, without creating . . .

LAURA: Give me a hug.

MARIA: Come here. You're not alone. You've come home. I'm not going to let anyone hurt you.

LAURA: Mama . . .

MARIA: Yes, I want to be your mama . . .

LAURA: Give me some of that.

MARIA: No. You're drinking too much.

LAURA: Just a little bit. As if it were a baby bottle . . .

MARIA: Here. Just a little bit. Okay, Laurie, okay . . .

LAURA: Are you happy?

MARIA: Now I am.

LAURA: I don't mean now. I mean before.

MARIA: No.

LAURA: Thanks.

MARIA: And you?

LAURA: I don't have any reason to be. I'm alone and I have nothing. It's been four years since I painted and eight since I've loved. I can't. I'm so miserable.

MARIA: I'll take care of you.

LAURA: I keep on dreaming of that son of a bitch every night. Those black eyes and the mole on his chest. And his strength that comes from not being a man in love.

MARIA: I'll make you forget him.

LAURA: He ruined my life. Just when I was beginning to make a name for myself, just when I was getting to be somebody, I had to leave everything and run away.

(Pause.)

MARIA: I'll make you forget him.

LAURA: Maria, men don't penetrate through the vagina. That's a lie. They penetrate some other place.

MARIA: Go to sleep.

LAURA: Some place that closes up and there's no way out. Where is the way out? Where?

MARIA (*Kissing her*): Easy . . . easy . . .

LAURA: I've gone to bed with so many guys. I've drunk so much. I've done so many things to love. I've had opportunities to forget. I must be crazy! I haven't been able to . . .

MARIA: I'm crazy, too. There's no hope for people in their right mind.

LAURA (*Without listening*): And I daydream about him, too. All my daydreams are wasted on our meeting. I close my eyes and imagine the scene: I ring the doorbell. There are footsteps, his footsteps. He opens the door. We look at each other. I'm wearing my red dress and he thinks I'm very beautiful. You can tell. He speaks: "Hi, Laura." I kiss him gently near his lips and he starts to tremble. Then he says, "I've been waiting eight years for this moment." (*Pause.*) Sometimes I meet him in the street, accidentally. We almost run into one another. In a revolving door . . . I don't know. (*Pause.*) And now I have him in the palm of my hand. And I can't! I'm afraid! I know it will turn out the way it always does.

MARIA: Forget him! Don't let him come between us.

LAURA: It's always the same. Men can want like brutes and there's nothing else. Nothing. Not a little drop of blood or a tear. Just semen . . . semen.

MARIA: Laura, forget him! Forget him!

LAURA: He was the one who did it best. My body was a pure caress against his body. My whole body was just a weak spot in his hands. Just his gentle rubbing was enough for me to feel everything. To understand that life was worth the effort. That's why I won't go. It's over.

MARIA: Yes, for God's sake, it's over!

LAURA: And if I see him I'll say: I don't want to kiss you anymore, or bite you. Don't come near me! (*She drinks.*) I want to put all of me in his mouth and caress him from inside. A final trip toward death. But no, I'm not going to rip his heart out.

MARIA: Laura, please! You're talking nonsense!

LAURA: That would be a sweet death. I'd say to his heart: Hello, my love. If I ripped his heart out, he'd still be alive.

MARIA: Laura!

LAURA: Then I'd go down into his guts. I'd find the hollow spot, I'd put my head there, and then, crack! A broken penis! A dead Juan!

MARIA: Please! Don't say such dreadful things! You're delirious. You're sick. Juan was . . . Juan is just a normal man.

LAURA: I wonder how he is?

MARIA: I know how he is. You see . . .

LAURA: His voice must be the same . . .

MARIA: Listen, I know things. I didn't go away. Life went on here for all of us. A long time after you ran away . . .

LAURA: I don't want to know!

MARIA: But you have to know. We have to get back to reality. One day . . .

LAURA: Can you imagine Juan being jealous on my account?

MARIA: Laura!

LAURA: What's wrong?
MARIA: You're not listening to me! I'm trying to tell you something . . .
LAURA: I won't see him. That is the only real death.
MARIA (*Shaking her*): Will you listen to me?
LAURA: And everything . . . for what?
MARIA: Juan . . .
LAURA: Don't even mention his name! (*Covering María's mouth. Gently.*) That man . . . (*She puts her hand to her heart.*) is gone from here now. (*MARIA shakes her head no.*) Don't tell me anything, I'm begging you. I don't want to know.
MARIA (*After a pause*): All right. If that's the way you want it. It's always the way you want it. Come.
LAURA: Where?
MARIA: I'm going to wash your pretty face.
LAURA (*Going toward the water, arm in arm with María*): Wash away my thoughts. Can you do that?
MARIA: I'll try. (*She sprinkles water on Laura's face and on her hair.*) How's that? How are those thoughts now?
LAURA: All scrambled and mixed up. Comb my hair, will you?
MARIA (*Laughing*): Sure. I'm going to make you look beautiful, really beautiful, just like a bride.

(*MARIA dries Laura's face. She combs her hair. She takes out a make-up case and puts eye shadow on Laura. LAURA cooperates.*)

MARIA: A bit of blue shadow . . . Like this. You still have elfin eyes.
LAURA: But now they're surrounded by wrinkles. See what you can do about them.
MARIA: You have a face worthy of you. Absolutely beautiful.
LAURA: Thank you. (*She looks María in the eyes.*) And why aren't you worthy of wrinkles?
MARIA (*Putting rouge on Laura*): You haven't looked at me carefully. When I laugh, or cry, or say the truth, there's no concealing them. Wrinkles are like ghosts, always trying to come out of their hiding places.
LAURA (*Laughing*): Are you going to cover up my ghosts?
MARIA: Just a bit of color. (*She puts red lipstick on Laura.*) You're much more beautiful like this. Beautiful like . . .
LAURA: A bride! Can you imagine two brides at the altar? Both in white silk. Both with veils covering their faces. And the priest saying, "Rosa, do you take Margarita as your lawfully wedded wife until death do you part? And you, Margarita, do you take Rosa as your lawfully wedded wife . . . ta ta tata . . . ta ta tata . . . ta ta ta ta ta . . .? And the priest, "You may kiss."

MARIA: And they both lift their veils, look at each other, and meld the red of their lips.

LAURA: And the guests asking one another: "Are you a friend of the bride or of the bride?

MARIA: And someone with a malicious mind murmuring, "They must be pregnant. They're both pregnant."

LAURA: And then the wedding dance begins. Can you see it? The two best men yield to the brides . . . dressed in white.

MARIA (*Putting a white sheet on Laura's head*): White like that on the outside. (*She puts on a sheet, too.*) White, white! (*She turns and dances. She puts on a record and we hear a waltz.*)

(*MARIA begins to dance with an imaginary man. LAURA gets up and follows her example. They both dance with their imaginary men. As they turn, they come face to face. They thank the best men and begin to dance together.*)

LAURA: And then?

MARIA: The brides take off their wedding gowns. (*She takes the sheets off them.*) And they meld the red of their lips. (*She slowly approaches Laura's mouth.*)

LAURA (*Pulling away*): María, did you get married in a wedding gown?

MARIA (*Catching her breath*): Yes, in white and in church.

LAURA: Good grief! What a hypocrite!

MARIA: Why?

LAURA: Oh, have you become a believer?

MARIA: It was a wonderful show. Nothing was missing. Even the priest was brilliant.

LAURA: And María Dehesa was the star actress.

MARIA: Yes, and so convincing that all day I believed it. I touched the guests' hearts. I made my parents happy. I was happy!

LAURA: You are such a fake.

MARIA: No way. The important part was there. The only essential ingredient was true.

LAURA: Love?

MARIA: Yes. I was in love with . . . the groom. We were both in love.

LAURA (*After a pause*): What's your husband like?

MARIA: He's . . . he's a man . . . (*She laughs.*) He's a man.

LAURA: And do you still love him?

MARIA: I think so.

LAURA: Does he treat you well?

MARIA: Well, he's not what he seemed to be. But none of us is what we seem when we're seducing each other. Now, sometimes he's a bit of a brute.

LAURA (*Laughing*): Really?
MARIA: I think he suffers a lot from the fact that I earn so much money.
LAURA: Why's that?
MARIA: I don't know. I think he feels. . .diminished. Men are not used to being. . . equal to women. Sometimes, without meaning to, he torments me and I think he'd like to see me fail. (*She laughs*.) And sometimes . . . he rapes me.
LAURA: Rapes you?
MARIA: It's just an expression. I pretend that I like it but while he penetrates me I count: one, two, three, four, five, six . . . I used to get to a hundred and fifteen, now it's twenty-one.
LAURA: Good God! And what do you do?
MARIA: Nothing. See, I'm living a routine, which amounts to the same thing as living reality.
LAURA: Not always.
MARIA: And what do you know . . . How many years have you seen the same man shave himself in your mirror?
LAURA: Until his beard poked me. From that moment on, it was goodbye.
MARIA: How romantic . . . ! Things are not the way you think. They're lots worse. At first, when you're with a man whose clothes are thrown on the floor of your room, and whose trouser belt is left next to the glass of spilled champagne, it's like the setting for a big party. And then, if the champagne makes it to the bedroom and falls on the floor, you go to get the mop so it doesn't ruin the wood, and on the way, you pick up his dirty underwear to stick 'em in the washing machine.
LAURA (*Affectionately*): That's just like you.
MARIA: There's nothing like living together to kill desire. It totally blows it away.
LAURA: You have to take care of desire. It's so fragile . . .
MARIA: My husband gets bad moods and kidney problems. And when he passes stones in his urine, he shows them to me and keeps them in the dresser as if they were gold nuggets. He demands his dinner on time and he can't miss a single soccer game. When I least expect it: (*Shouting*.) Goal! (*LAURA jumps*.) That's what used to happen to me. He suffers from insomnia and insists that I sing him lullabies so he can sleep . . .
LAURA: Why don't you get a divorce?
MARIA: You don't understand. I can't explain it. If you set all that aside, my husband is a faithful, handsome, intelligent man.
LAURA: Yes, but you don't desire him. You don't even like him.
MARIA: And what does that matter to me? I have my own life. I assure you that it's not easy either tolerating somebody else's success. Do you know what Durrell says? That lovers are never well matched. That there's always one who projects a shadow over the other, preventing that one's growth, so that the one who

remains in the shadow is always tormented by the desire to escape, to feel free and so to grow.

LAURA: And why doesn't he escape?

MARIA: Because he has chosen to love.

LAURA: And you?

MARIA: (*With sadness*): To be a shadow.

LAURA: Hey, hey, don't look so sad.

MARIA: No, no. Oh, what a mess . . . It's so hot . . . it's so hot!

LAURA (*Sprinkling water on Maria*): At least we have water. Water, water! Come on, let's see you smile!

(*They both splash water on themselves. MARIA hugs Laura with a certain anguish.*)

MARIA: I'm so happy you're here. So happy . . .

LAURA (*Drawing away*): I'm hungry.

MARIA: I made you chocolate pie with whipped cream.

LAURA: Bring it out, Mama.

MARIA: You know I don't like it when you call me mama.

LAURA: Do you remember when my mother died? I was brokenhearted. You were a little girl, just like me. Then one night, you braided my hair, a long, tight braid, and I thought: how well my mama does it, and I began to love you.

MARIA: And to use me.

LAURA: Because you liked it.

MARIA: I did not like it.

LAURA: You liked to make my bed in the dormitory and later to be my guard when we had our apartment.

MARIA: And you liked to have a maid. A maid who did the housework while the lady did her art.

LAURA: You taught me a lot about discipline. Later on I forgot it.

MARIA: Yes. I admired you so much . . . ! And you wiped out all of my canvases with a glance.

LAURA: Honey, they were bad.

MARIA: Time has said otherwise.

LAURA: Don't tell me you believe that? That crap they've been telling you?

MARIA: You're in no position to pull irony on me.

LAURA (*Picking up a painting*): You like this, really?

MARIA: I like yours better. Those invisible paintings that are flooding the galleries.

LAURA: I'm honest. I could never sell garbage.

MARIA: You didn't have me and you went to hell.

LAURA: I left you. And you resent me for it. Give me my glass, please. If I don't get drunk, I can't stand you. You know? Sometimes when I drink a lot I paint. If you give me some more, I'll show you.
MARIA (*Handing her the bottle*): Here. Go on destroying yourself if you want to.
LAURA: And you, go on enjoying it . . . (*She drinks.*)
MARIA: Why do we always have to fight? We're grown up now.
LAURA: No. I see us as being the same as before. (*She laughs.*) How funny! I feel as if I'm in a time warp.
MARIA: Do you want some pie?
LAURA: You criticize me for the very things you thrive on.
MARIA (*Angrily*): Do you want some pie?
LAURA: Have you put my name on top in chocolate?

(*MARIA opens the refrigerator and takes out the pie.*)

LAURA: Feed it to me with a spoon.
MARIA (*Throwing the pie in her face*): Here, have a spoonful.
LAURA (*Laughing*): You've got me all dirty. You've messed me up.
MARIA: You make a delightful picture.
LAURA: A picture? Yes, let's paint. I do feel like painting. Now I'll paint you. I'll paint your body, like when we were little. I like your body in colors. (*She takes paint and smears Maria's legs.*)
MARIA: Let me alone. If you want to paint, I'll give you a canvas.
LAURA: I want you to be my canvas.
MARIA: I don't want to.
LAURA: Why?
MARIA: I don't want us to be little again. I don't want to be your old rag. I don't want you to mess me up.
LAURA: You started it.
MARIA: So what?
LAURA: You used to like it. (*She goes after Maria with the paint.*)
MARIA: Now I don't.
LAURA: Now, too. You were having fun.
MARIA: Because it was the only time you looked at me.
LAURA: Take off your shirt.
MARIA: But . . .
LAURA: I'm inspired.
MARIA: Take off your dress. I'm inspired, too.
LAURA: You? You don't know how.
MARIA (*Going over to Laura and unbuttoning her with a yank*): We'll see about that.

LAURA (*Giving Maria a paintbrush*): Here, bitch.
MARIA (*Tossing the paintbrush away*): With our hands.
LAURA (*Dipping her hands in red and painting Maria's abdomen*): Hell. Hell is the empty womb. (*She presses her hands against Maria's abdomen. MARIA complains softly.*) The red of sterility. Sterile womb at thirty-five.
MARIA (*Painting large black stripes on Laura's body*): Jail! Frustration hides itself behind the bars. Failure.
LAURA (*Going faster, using yellow*): A sun on each breast. With great black clouds on the nipples.
MARIA: Rust colors for autumn. The falling leaves.
LAURA: Garbage in the belly button of my jailer. You killed me, you killed me!
MARIA (*From behind Laura*): Pink tones on your back and the green of screams. A dickey bird lands on your ass. Do you have lovers?
LAURA: Yes, yes, yes . . .
MARIA: They're all dead! (*Her painting of Laura is violent.*) All dead!
LAURA: Mauve and purple. The color of frigid women who only have orgasms in their dreams.
MARIA (*Painting Laura in fury*): But I can still fake it! I still have someone to fake it with! And you?
LAURA (*Painting Maria's face*): Faker! Faker!
MARIA (*Quickly*): And you? And you?
LAURA: Lovers are something else. (*Frantically.*) If they don't do it well, they don't come back the next day. I may not love, but I enjoy.
MARIA: Whore!
LAURA: Faker!
MARIA: Whore! Filthy bitch!

(*They paint each other madly, almost hurting each other.*)

LAURA: Whore. Pig. Liar.
MARIA: Faker. Faker!

(*They start to hit each other only to end up in a desperate hug. Their colors run together.*)

MARIA: Why did you have to fall in love like some idiot? We had it all.
LAURA: All but the most important thing.
MARIA: You left and took away all the ideas, all the water. You left me empty.
LAURA: And I lost it all.
MARIA: Why did you leave?
LAURA: You already know.

MARIA: We had a treasure clutched between two hands. One was yours and one was mine. You've seen. Without me you were nothing. I . . . I was your hand. Have you come back?
LAURA (*Pulling away*): I don't want to give you any explanations.
MARIA: I wanted to be your hand.
LAURA: I didn't want it. You were suffocating me. I think . . . That night, who told Juan that . . . ?
MARIA: I didn't.
LAURA: You were determined that he should leave me. You couldn't stand the thought . . .
MARIA: He made you sick. You were dying.
LAURA: So you arranged everything. But it turned out bad.
MARIA: Juan did not love you.
LAURA: What in the hell difference did it make to you? You didn't give me a chance to fight.
MARIA: Don't go on fooling yourself. You never mattered in the least to Juan. You were just the easiest bitch he could find.

(*LAURA spits in Maria's face. MARIA crumbles.*)

LAURA: Forgive me. My God, we're crazy. Forgive me. I'm drunk. Please, don't do this . . .
MARIA: It hurts so much . . . It hurts so much . . .
LAURA: What does?
MARIA: Here, here, everywhere. My insides.
LAURA: Look, look. The paint's running down your face from the tears. What a pretty picture! Come, look at yourself in the mirror. (*MARIA cries in front of the mirror.*) Now your face is the earthly paradise.
MARIA: No. You're hurting me. Can't you give me something?
LAURA: No. I'm sorry, but I can't.
MARIA: Why? I can help you.
LAURA: It just can't be.

(*MARIA, furious, draws the screen on the fountain shut, with herself inside. We hear the sound of the water.*)

LAURA: Maria!
MARIA (*From inside, drily*): What?
LAURA: Life's a bitch, isn't it?
MARIA: Yes.

LAURA: If you and I were a man and a woman, we'd be happy. (*Ironic laughter from MARIA.*) Why are you laughing?

MARIA: We'd destroy one another.

LAURA: No.

MARIA: We've already destroyed one another as two women.

LAURA: We destroy one another because we're not a man and a woman.

MARIA (*Reappearing*): You can have the shower. (*LAURA gets in the shower and closes it.*)

MARIA (*Returning to her tone at the beginning*): In any event, I want to give you a hand. I have a lot of friends. A lot of important people who'll appreciate your talent. Where do you live?

LAURA: In a boardinghouse.

MARIA: I've an empty apartment in the center of town. My old studio. You can go live there. Until you find something, I'll give you money. It's no big deal for me you know. I'll drop by once in a while to see what you're doing. And, well, if you want to pay me back in some way, I do need a model. You'd only have to come two afternoons a week. Tuesday and Thursday, say. That's only if you want to pay me back in some way. It's not necessary. You have to get some new clothes. One's image really counts. And, of course, you have to stop drinking and . . .

LAURA (*Opening the screen*): Where's the towel.

MARIA: You can move right away, tomorrow. There's a bed in the studio, and art supplies. (*LAURA gets dressed.*) If you need something, you call me and ask. (*LAURA picks up her handbag.*) Where are you going?

LAURA: Home.

MARIA: Now?

LAURA: Yes.

MARIA: We have to make arrangements . . .

LAURA: No way.

MARIA: What are you saying?

LAURA: I'm not going to your studio.

MARIA: Why?

LAURA: Because I'm not, that's all; because I'm not.

MARIA: Forget your pride.

LAURA (*Shaking her head*): Listen, I appreciate it, really, but . . .

MARIA: Okay. (*She makes out a check and signs it.*) Here, take it.

LAURA (*She takes it, looks at it, and tears it up*): Thanks.

MARIA: You'd rather have the bedbugs eat you up. You'd rather starve to death than have me . . .

LAURA: Yes. I'm not as sick as you think. Seeing you has consoled me. Money, good health, love . . . Success, no. No. Do you understand?

MARIA: You're a masochist.
LAURA: But I still have my self-respect. I'm not for sale. Goodbye.
MARIA (*Falling on her knees*): Not like this. You can't leave me like this.
LAURA: I'm not up for any more little scenes. I just want to sleep.
MARIA: Ask me for something. Even if it's just one little thing. Can I give you something?
LAURA: No.
MARIA: My friendship.
LAURA: No.
MARIA: Why?
LAURA: You expect too much of me and I have nothing to give in exchange.
MARIA: I don't want anything in exchange.
LAURA: I don't want to hurt you any more.
MARIA: I swear. Not anything. I don't want anything.
LAURA (*Touching her affectionately*): I'm leaving.

(*MARIA gets up in a flash and blocks the door.*)

MARIA: No.
LAURA: I'm very tired.
MARIA: Don't go.
LAURA: Would you please let me out the door?
MARIA: No.
LAURA: Don't be ridiculous.
MARIA: You're not going to humiliate me any more. (*She locks the door.*) Now you can't leave.
LAURA: What are you trying to do?
MARIA: You have to stay here until you know everything.
LAURA: Open that door.
MARIA: No way.
LAURA (*Trying to take the keys away from Maria. They struggle*): Give me the keys.

(*MARIA runs and grabs a scissors. She waves it at Laura.*)

MARIA: If you don't do what I say, I'll kill you. I swear!
LAURA (*Going over to Maria*): Come on, don't talk nonsense.
MARIA: Don't come near me. Sit down over there!
LAURA: What's wrong with you?
MARIA: Sit down on that chair!
LAURA: Have you gone crazy?

MARIA (*Raising her hand*): Now sit on that chair or I'll kill you. I'm warning you. I'm waiting for the chance.

(*LAURA sits down. MARIA gets a cord and a rag.*)

MARIA: Do it. Put your hands behind you.
LAURA: Maria . . .
MARIA: Shut up!

(*LAURA obeys. MARIA starts to tie her up.*)

LAURA (*Softly*): Maria, this is crazy . . .
MARIA: Now it's your turn to look, to listen, to be quiet for a while. (*She gags Laura.*) You've been asking for it, Laura dear. You came to humiliate me, to trample on me like when we were . . . like always. Don't move! I have a big surprise for you. (*She looks at Laura.*) Laurie, how insignificant you are, like that. (*She holds Laura by the throat.*) When your serpent's mouth is shut. (*She squeezes Laura's throat but ends up caressing her.*) I'm not killing you because that would be doing you a favor. Because there's one thing that has meaning for you. That shadow that hasn't let you grow, that's turned you into a dwarf. Just hold still, Laurie, I'm going to perform magic for you. I'm going to leave you alone with him.

(*MARIA turns out the light and puts on the answering machine.*)

JUAN'S VOICE (*From offstage*): Maria! Maria! Are you there? Listen, honey, don't wait supper for me. I've got to work late. Everything okay? See you tonight. Love ya.

(*MARIA enters and turns on the light.*)

MARIA: Juan is my husband. (*LAURA stares at her fixedly.*) He's mine. Say that it's so. (*LAURA moves her head slightly. She is frozen. MARIA takes the gag away.*) Speak up. (*LAURA remains silent.*) Aren't you going to say anything? (*LAURA does not answer.*) Checkmate. (*MARIA unties Laura. Silence.*) Come on. Say something. (*LAURA smiles at her.*) Don't do that. (*LAURA caresses her.*) Hit me. Kill me. I . . . I fell in love with him when you went away. I fell desperately in love. What could I do? Say something, please. Insult me, at least. Say that I'm evil, that I'm . . . (*In a desperate scream.*) I tried to tell you before. You didn't let me! Say something!
LAURA: Thanks.
MARIA: Not that.

(*LAURA takes a letter out of her purse and holds it out to Maria.*)

LAURA: Read this.
MARIA (*She does not take it*): What is it?
LAURA: It's from your husband. (*Pause.*)
MARIA: What does he tell you?
LAURA (*Taking the letter out of the envelope and reading*): Madrid. August 1, ____. (*LAURA supplies current year.*)
MARIA: You haven't seen him yet?
LAURA: No. Open the door.
MARIA: Why haven't you gone?
LAURA: I couldn't think things through clearly.
MARIA: Are you going to go?
LAURA: Do I have your permission? (*Pause.*)
MARIA: He looks handsome. More handsome than ever. And, sometimes, I think he stills smells of you.
LAURA: Will you let me see him this time?
MARIA: Sure. You should go tonight. (*She gets out the keys.*)
LAURA: But he'll want to go to bed with me.
MARIA: Go ahead.
LAURA: And I won't count: one, two, three, four, five . . . I won't count, Maria.
MARIA: So much the better.
LAURA: Maybe you've made him impotent.
MARIA (*Opening the door*): Find out for yourself. Go on, it's your turn. Maybe after a good screw you'll get your inspiration back.
LAURA: Never, dear. I'll never take anything that's part yours. (*Pause.*) Thank you for clearing up a little doubt of mine . . . for lending me your perspective. Thank you. (*She is about to leave but turns and points to the canvas.*) Oh, by the way, the hands have to be hers. No, it doesn't matter that she has no arms. It's something like . . . That's it! Wait a minute! (*Quickly.*) The figure in a downward motion trying to reach the lock with her mouth. The bird looking up with an open beak. (*At top speed.*) The light, only from behind. A white light. And on the floor. . . pieces of broken body . . . stains. (*Pause.*) It's just an idea.
MARIA (*Softly*): I hate you. I hate you with all my soul.
LAURA: I don't hate you. (*LAURA exits. MARIA slowly crosses to the bird. She opens the cage. The bird flies out.*)

THE END

Maria Maberino and Michael Calderon in the American premiere of *A Night Divided*, 1991, at Pace University in New York City. Directed by Timur Djordjadze. Producion design by Christopher Thomas.

A NIGHT DIVIDED

CHARACTERS

Sabina Garcia, an actress
Alberto Guzman, a Bible salesman
Jean-Luc, Sabina's lover

The terrace of a top-floor apartment in Madrid. We can see the little windows of the taller buildings, television antennas, clotheslines, etc. The terrace is filled with plants. Center stage, a table with folding chairs and a plum tree with large red leaves. Also a hammock and a mirror against the wall.

It is nightfall on a September evening.

SABINA enters with a bottle and a full glass in her hand. She is a beautiful woman, about twenty-five years old. She is slender and shapely. Her skin is smooth, like a green apple. She is singing in a wavering voice, inebriated and sad.

She sets the bottle and glass on the table and exits. We hear her singing from inside the apartment. She returns, carrying a telephone that she puts on the table, and a script that she glances over for a moment. She drinks and then refills the glass. She gets up and positions herself in front of the mirror.

SABINA (*Acting*): Leave me alone! Let go of me, you beast! Don't touch me I said! (*She makes the gesture of giving someone the knee.*) That's right, that's right. Squirm like a little lizard. No, that's not it. (*She looks at the script and takes a drink.*) That's right, that's the way I like to see you, squirming like a slimy reptile. (*Thinking.*) Do reptiles squirm? It doesn't matter . . . (*She continues.*) Squirm like a slimy reptile! You asked for it. Who said you could pawn my gold watch? The only thing I had to remember my grandmother by. Don't say anything! Don't talk to me! And all for what? That's a lie! All to pay for the whims of that bitch you're sleeping with. (*Changing her tone.*) All to pay for the whims of that bitch you're sleeping with. (*Changing her tone.*) All to pay for the whims of that bitch you're sleeping with. (*She takes a drink and continues.*) No, don't talk to me! I don't want to hear you! Pack your suitcase and get out of my house right now. I've told you I don't want your explanations. (*She drinks and reads the script.*) I don't believe your fantastic stories anymore. You say you love me? Ha, ha, ha. (*Beat.*) The only thing you love is my money, you pig. (*She reads the script and drinks.*) My money, you pig. But get up off the floor, you rat, you look like a worm. Aren't you ashamed? (*She reads the script.*) Aldo, my little lion. I thought you would be the last man in my life. That you would eclipse all of your rivals and pred . . . prede . . . predecessors. I had dreamed of going to your funeral as a little old lady and crying over you. (*She spits.*) That's what you deserve. What are you doing? Why are you looking at me like that? Come on, Aldo, it was all just a joke, my turtledove. Don't do anything foolish, and let go of that knife. (*She turns her head suddenly toward the telephone and picks it up.*) Hello? Hello? Yes? Anybody there? (*She hangs up and takes another drink.*) It was all just a joke, my turtledove. Don't do anything foolish, and let go of that knife. (*She shrinks back.*) Aldo . . . Aldo! (*She lets out a moan and falls.*) I knew you would be my last. (*She dies.*) How dreadful! It's awful . . . ! My turtledove, my turtledove . . . What crap. (*The doorbell rings. Startled, SABINA gets up off the floor and picks up the telephone.*) Hello, honey. Hello! Hello! (*The doorbell sounds again. SABINA hangs up and exits, wobbling, to open the door.*)

ALBERTO (*Offstage*): May I please speak to the head of the house?

SABINA (*Offstage*): Come in, come in. Don't be shy. I'm all alone. My house is your house. (*She enters with ALBERTO.*) My terrace is your terrace. And the sky up above is your sky, too, okay?

(*ALBERTO nods timidly. He is a young man who appears a bit gauche but nice. His hair is greased and combed back. He has on a tie that's no longer in style and a threadbare summer jacket. He wears glasses. He is holding a heavy briefcase.*)

SABINA: Well sit down, don't be shy. You're just in time to kill me. You know? It's difficult to die alone, without anybody to stab you. (*She hands him something from the table.*) Here. Stab me with this. (*ALBERTO gets up.*) Don't be frightened, man, just stab me gently. Look, like this. (*ALBERTO objects.*) Did I hurt you?

ALBERTO: No ma'am, but . . .

SABINA: Dying is what actors like to do best. It's such pleasure, to be able to squirm, to make faces, and then . . . Plop! You expire. It's the only thing I like in this stupid sequence. The rest is a dreadful scene, zoophilous . . . Is that how you say it?

ALBERTO: What?

SABINA: That . . . when you use a lot of animals. (*Emphatically.*) You look like a rat!

ALBERTO: Pardon me.

SABINA: It's a metaphor, man. Just pig or just rat, no. But, for example, you squirm like a slimy reptile, that's a metaphor, isn't it?

ALBERTO: Yes ma'am, that's exactly right. Life itself is a metaphor. (*He takes a Bible from the briefcase.*) And the Bible is the book of metaphors par excellence. I believe that you love metaphors.

SABINA: Me? No!

ALBERTO: Perhaps then, signs and symbols . . . Well it's all condensed right here. Ma'am, I come to offer you the book of books. The only philosophy that will last for the centuries.

SABINA: Why are you calling me ma'am? I'm not so old . . . How old do you think I am?

ALBERTO: Oh . . . twenty, twenty-one at most. The ideal age for starting to understand what's in here.

SABINA: Twenty-one? That's it; I'm twenty-one. (*Throwing down the script.*) And this role's not right for me. It's not right! Can you imagine me married to a lizard who pawns my jewelry and plays around behind my back with some bitch? And to top it off, the bitch is the lead role. That's the worst of all. They talk and talk about me, but I don't appear. I finally come out at the end so they can see me be killed. It's absurd! I can't relate to this character. I can't find any reality in common. I have no jewels. I, I . . . (*Suddenly.*) Did the phone ring?

ALBERTO: I didn't hear anything.

SABINA (*Picking up the phone*): Hello? Hello? (*She hangs up, disappointed again.*) I'm waiting for a call. (*She drinks.*) He calls me every Tuesday, you know. What time is it?

ALBERTO (*Nervously*): Eight-thirty.

SABINA: Eight-thirty already! He has to call any minute now. (*She drinks.*) Excuse me, would you like a drink?

ALBERTO: No thank you. I don't drink.

SABINA: You don't drink? I normally don't either, but . . . Tonight's different. Sometimes you have to drink in order to see things differently . . . more realistically, you understand? Because . . . Who am I really? Or who are you, really? Who are you?

ALBERTO: A sales representative for The Light, Inc. The only company exclusively dedicated . . .

SABINA: No. Who am I? The normal me or the drunk me? Alcohol provokes lucidity, it activates the sluggish brain, and it takes us to the limits of our authentic needs. Lonely people drink in order to talk to themselves in the mirror. Shy people to be able to look. And cowards in order . . . cowards in order to act. That's it! That's why I drink. Champagne to bring a story to an end! (*She drinks.*) It's good, would you like a glass?

ALBERTO: No, really. I don't drink . . . during work hours. I only wanted to steal five minutes of your time in order to . . .

SABINA: Steal five minutes? You don't have to steal, I'll give them to you. I'll give you five minutes and a glass of champagne. I'll go get it.

ALBERTO: Don't bother.

(*SABINA pays no attention to him and goes to get a glass. In the meantime, ALBERTO starts taking different kinds of Bibles out of the suitcase and puts them on the table. SABINA returns with a glass. She fills the glass, spilling some on a book that ALBERTO picks up and quickly wipes clean.*)

SABINA: You must think that I'm crazy or frivolous, right? But that's a lie. I believe in God.

ALBERTO (*Beaming*): That's exactly what I came to talk to you about, if you will grant me . . .

SABINA: What's wrong is that I'm drunk.

ALBERTO: That's not a problem. You yourself just said that alcohol provokes lucidity. There are things that cannot be appreciated if . . .

SABINA (*Interrupting him again*): It's all because I'm in love. Yes, I'm totally and desperately in love with a phantom who calls me on Tuesdays . . . that's today. So that my voice doesn't tremble, I drink a little bit. I usually just drink a little bit, like this, you know? But today's different because I've reached a decision.

ALBERTO: Perhaps a hasty one.

SABINA: Hasty? What do you know? I should have made this decision a year ago, when he went back to his country. And you, who know nothing, call me hasty . (Pause.)

ALBERTO: Please don't be angry, ma'am. I only . . .

SABINA: If you call me "ma'am" one more time, we're through talking. We'll cut off communication, completely. Do you hear?

ALBERTO: Let me explain. When I said "hasty," that was because sometimes one needs help before making an important decision. You understand. We live in a world filled with rushing and anguish. We're always overburdened with petty things and we forget the most fundamental. The great truths of life. Have you read the Bible?

SABINA: What's it to you? If you want to make me feel ignorant, if besides feeling drunk, stupid, and abandoned, if besides all that you want me to . . .

ALBERTO: Of course not. If you don't yet have a Bible, that means nothing. That's why I'm here. There's a special offer this month. Something really exceptional. This volume, for example, bound in leather, that normally sells for $250, we're offering it, this month only, for the low low price of $209.99.

SABINA (*Picking up the telephone*): Yes? Hello? (*She hangs up and looks at Alberto.*) Nobody there.

ALBERTO: I can assure you that it's a real bargain. A special opportunity! Besides, we have them in almost every color. We 're always thinking about the customer and what blends with the decor. When I came in, I noticed your pine furniture--and very attractive it is, too--and either the green or the brown would go marvelously . . .

SABINA: I can't . . . I'm not going to be able to . . . !

ALBERTO: We also have economical ones. (*He looks for a different one*.)

SABINA: Once I hear his voice I just won't be able to and I'll be like the little dwarf in *Snow White*. Mute. (*She laughs*.)

ALBERTO (*Laughing, without understanding*): This one, for example, a classic style, costs only $180.

SABINA: A hundred and eighty miserable dollars is what they're paying me for tomorrow's session.

ALBERTO: Ma'am . . .

SABINA (*Yelling*): What?

ALBERTO: Excuse me, I don't know what to call you.

SABINA: Me?

ALBERTO: What's your name?

SABINA: The real one? My real name?

ALBERTO: Whatever one you like.

SABINA: Sabina Garcia.

ALBERTO (*Getting up and holding out his hand*): Alberto Guzman. Pleased to meet you.

SABINA (*Without noticing him, she pours herself another drink*): I don't like Sabina. It doesn't fit me. It would go with a tall woman whose hair is almost white with white eyebrows and blue, almost white eyes. That's why I've changed my name. My professional name is Venus Vega. But you can call me Sabina, okay?

ALBERTO: It sounds familiar. I must have seen you in the movies.

SABINA: Can I confess something to you? I warn you it's something very sad. Hey, you. What are you thinking about?

ALBERTO: I was thinking about your session tomorrow. It would be . . . it would be so symbolic if you invested your session in me.

SABINA: In you?

ALBERTO: If you bought a Bible from me. On installments, of course.

SABINA: Everything's on installments these days. Even love is on the installment plan.

ALBERTO: I haven't sold one all day.

SABINA: Love on the installment plan. Jean-Luc promises me every Tuesday that he'll come the next week and he never does. But today I'm going to tell him it's all over. (*She laughs sadly.*) And to top it off, he wants me to be faithful, faithful . . . (*Serious.*) And I am faithful because. . . I love him. (*While Sabina talks, ALBERTO is working out some calculations.*) Today I swear to you that I'm going to tell him it's all over. I can't take it anymore! And you will be the silent witness to my sorrow. What are you doing? You're not listening to me. . .

ALBERTO (*Startled*): Excuse me, but . . . You don't listen to me either. And my time is as important as yours. And we both have our problems.

SABINA: What have you written there?

ALBERTO: Are you interested?

SABINA: Yes.

ALBERTO: Look, if you pay for it in a year it comes to $17.50 a month, less five percent.

SABINA: You're a monster. For even one second you can't forget your . . . You, you have to be something more than you and those fat books . . .

ALBERTO: I'm very sorry, Sabina, but if I don't sell one this evening . . . Well, I believe my problems don't interest you.

SABINA: How much did you say that one costs?

ALBERTO: In installments or for cash?

SABINA: What is it? (*She picks it up.*) Oh, they're Bibles. So you sell Bibles? That's the way life is. You meet a stranger and then you find out that you have a bunch of things in common. Before I became an actress I used to sell Bibles door to door, too. Finally they fired me because I was so bad at it. To get even, I kept all the ones I had at home. Want to see 'em? I've got at least fifteen.

ALBERTO (*Downcast*): No, no, forget it. I believe you. But you could have said so right away.

SABINA: You didn't ask.

ALBERTO: I asked you if you had read it and you said no.

SABINA: Well I haven't read it. (*ALBERTO starts to pick up his books.*) Say, what's your name?

ALBERTO: Alberto Guzman. (*He takes out his card.*)

SABINA: Shit! You can't forget your profession for one second. You got your head that wrapped up in it?

ALBERTO: When I don't sell anything, yes. I'm sorry, Sabina, but I have to keep working.

SABINA: Come on, have a drink with me.

ALBERTO: I'd love to, but . . .

SABINA: Please . . . I don't want to be alone. Am I that impossible to be around?

ALBERTO: Not at all, but if I don't sell a Bible this evening, they'll fire me.

SABINA: It would be good for you. You're getting very skinny.

ALBERTO: I know, but I have a mother and four brothers and sisters, and besides that. . .

SABINA: Really? I have seven. I have seven wonderful rays of sunshine. And I'd like to have seven children, but the problem is I don't have a husband. Listen, did the phone ring?

ALBERTO: Don't pick it up. It didn't ring. (*He looks at his watch.*) Well, I'm really sorry but . . . (*He crosses to the exit. In the doorway, SABINA grabs him.*)

SABINA: Don't go. If you stay, I'll buy it.

ALBERTO: No, no . . . You have lots of them.

SABINA: What difference does that make?

ALBERTO: Seriously, forget it. I still have time to try some place else.

SABINA: Don't be stubborn.

ALBERTO: I can't sell it to you. Business is business, but . . .

SABINA: In cash, and you stay.

ALBERTO: No, no. You already have fifteen of them. I'm not out to rob you.

SABINA (*Taking his briefcase away from him*): Let me pick out one I don't have. Let's see. This green binding is very . . .

ALBERTO (*Automatically*): It goes very well with your shelves.

SABINA: What?

ALBERTO: Nothing. I didn't say a word. It's occupational warping.

SABINA: Seriously, does that work for you?

ALBERTO: It certainly . . . doesn't.

SABINA: I never had the nerve to try it. It's a bit much, don't you think? Look, I'll buy this one--with the black cover to match my heart. (*She laughs.*) How much is it?

ALBERTO: No, really. Tomorrow you'll regret it. You're not in any shape . . .

SABINA: Nor are you, to say no. Don't be silly. You save your job and I cope with my fear. Don't you think that's enough to make up for losing our dignity?

ALBERTO (*After a pause, he takes off his glasses*): Yes.

SABINA: Okay, then. Now, while we're waiting, we'll both drink. (*She fills the glasses. ALBERTO raises his.*) No, before you drink, you have to make a wish.

ALBERTO: A wish?

SABINA: Yes.

ALBERTO (*Thinking*): Okay. And you?

SABINA: Okay. Bottoms up. (*They drink.*) What did you ask for?

ALBERTO: I can't tell you.

SABINA: Why not?

ALBERTO: Just can't.

SABINA: Sure you can. Come on.

ALBERTO (*After a pause*): That the phone ring.

SABINA: Yes, let it ring for heaven's sake. I have it all rehearsed. I know every word I'm going to say. And I'm going to ask him to give me back my keys. That's symbolic, isn't it? Because when you love something or somebody there are no excuses that mean anything. I'd leave everything for him. (*She looks at Alberto.*) Are you in love?

ALBERTO: I don't know.

SABINA: If you don't know, then you're not. And you won't be able to understand anything I tell you.

ALBERTO: Don't worry. I'm not as stupid as I look.

SABINA: Look, when I talk to him my hands shake. When I walk through the streets, I see him at every corner. I mistake the trees for him. When I put on music, I hear his voice. And that's not the worst of it. The worst of it is that it keeps me from seeing. I've been drinking today because otherwise I couldn't tell him. Today the story's going to be over. The End. *Fini*.

ALBERTO: Why?

SABINA: Why? Can't you figure it out?

ALBERTO: He doesn't love you.

SABINA: If he loved me, he'd come. He'd open my door and he'd get in my bed. Wouldn't you do that for the woman you love? Wouldn't you?

ALBERTO: But sometimes . . . I don't know. What I was thinking is all wet, because if I were he, I wouldn't have any doubts.

(*ALBERTO drinks nervously.*)

SABINA: Why did you look at me like that? Are you feeling sorry for me?

ALBERTO: Sorry? You're an angel . . .

SABINA (*Laughing*): An angel from the Bible?

ALBERTO: No! An angel woman. A beautiful woman. A desirable angel.

SABINA: And what are you like? I can't see you very well.

ALBERTO: It's getting dark.

SABINA (*Crying*): And he doesn't call! He doesn't even call anymore. (*She bangs on the telephone.*) Ring, dammit. Ring already! I'm ready. Jean-Luc. (*Beat.*) Jean-Luc . . . You're going to hear about all the pain you've caused me.

ALBERTO: Calm down, we're going to have you calm down. Here, would you like a cigarette?

SABINA (*Lighting it*): I'm the one who's going to leave him. He has to let me do it. Do you know what? With him I've never made even one decision. He calls, and I go; he pushes me aside, and I go away. He kisses me, and I give myself to him. And that isn't right, is it? And do you know why it isn't right? Because in the long run, you're afraid. You feel defenseless, fragile. And when you're afraid a long time, you get sad, and men don't like sad women. Do you like women?

ALBERTO: Some of them.

SABINA: Sad women?

ALBERTO: I only like a sad woman when I can make her happy.

SABINA: You see? That's egotistical. I always like Jean-Luc. I like to look at him from far away when he's sad. I like it when he cries. When Jean-Luc cries, I lick his tears and they taste heavenly, like good wine, like nectar, like ambrosia. But I must be boring you.

ALBERTO: Not at all. I feel like I've entered the movie screen. And it's not a dream; it's all real. Tell me where the light is. I want to see you better.

(*We hear cats howling. ALBERTO turns on the light and leans on the terrace railing.*)

ALBERTO: How pretty everything seems from here. Come, look at all the cats on the rooftops. They come out at night to find each other.

SABINA (*Putting her hand on his shoulder*): Cats don't have mates. They get involved when they feel like it and they don't lie to each other.

ALBERTO: And when they're wounded, they lick themselves with their pretty little pink tongues.

SABINA: They do their own thing. They're like us but they don't deceive themselves. No one knows anyone. (*Suddenly she runs to the telephone but does not take it off the hook. Pause. She stares at Alberto in a strange way.*)

ALBERTO: Why are you looking at me like that?

SABINA (*While still staring at him*): He doesn't even call me any more. (*Pause. Seductively.*) What did you say that cats do?

ALBERTO: When?

SABINA: When they find each other on the rooftops.

ALBERTO: They chase each other and circle around each other.

SABINA: They dance?

ALBERTO: Something like that.

SABINA: Do you dance?

ALBERTO: Me?

(*SABINA fills his glass and gives it to him. Then she exits and returns with an old record player and a record. She puts it on.*)

SABINA: Now I'm your kitty cat.

(*ALBERTO starts to circle around her. They get more and more lively and dance uninhibitedly. It's a war dance filled with eroticism. Without stopping her dancing, SABINA fills his glass.*)

SABINA: Drink. I want you to be as drunk as I am.
ALBERTO (*Drinking*): Let's lose our heads!
SABINA: Let's lose consciousness! Meow, meow, meow . . .
ALBERTO: Meow, meow, meow . . .

(*They laugh.*)

SABINA (*Down on all fours*): Grab hold of me. Catch me.
ALBERTO (*Crawling after her on the floor*): Don't run. I can smell you. I want you.
SABINA (*Getting away*): Here, kitty, kitty. Come on. (*She purrs.*)
ALBERTO (*Grabbing her*): You're making me hot. I'm going to eat you. (*He kisses her.*)

(*ALBERTO starts to unbutton her blouse. SABINA starts to cry.*)

ALBERTO: What's wrong? Why are you crying?
SABINA: I can't. He . . . he'd never forgive me.
ALBERTO: Forget him. Don't you see that he's not here?
SABINA: I can't. I just can't.
ALBERTO: Weren't you going to leave him?
SABINA: Yes. I swear to you it's all over!
ALBERTO: Well? Actions speak louder than words.
SABINA (*After a pause*): Get me another drink.
ALBERTO: Why?
SABINA: So we can lose our heads completely.

(*ALBERTO refills the glasses and they both drink it straight down.*)

SABINA: What's your name?
ALBERTO: Alberto.
SABINA: Alberto, I love you.
ALBERTO: You're gorgeous.
SABINA: Stroke my back and tell me sweet things.

(*SABINA turns around and ALBERTO caresses her.*)

ALBERTO: Sweet things. Sweet things. Sweet things. That's right. Laugh. Laugh. You have the most beautiful back I've ever touched in my life. That's right, my wild little cat, purr, purr. What a beautiful path I've found! I wonder where it goes? Oh . . . I'm dying . . .

SABINA: Are you as drunk as I am or less?

ALBERTO: I'm drunk from you. I'm beginning to hallucinate. Let me look at you. (*He looks at her.*) Beautiful, beautiful, beautiful . . .

SABINA: Do you love me?

ALBERTO: You drive me crazy.

SABINA: Say it to me again. It's been so long since I've heard it.

ALBERTO: I love you so much. I want you. I'm going to eat . . . I love you. I love you.

SABINA: How much? How much?

ALBERTO: You'll see. (*He lights his cigarette lighter and sets fire to a Bible.*)

SABINA: What are you doing?

ALBERTO: Answering you. Now all the angels are in hell. (*He drinks from the bottle.*) Goodbye, St. Paul. Goodbye, St. John. Goodbye, St. Matthew. Alberto Guzman condemns you to the flames to purify his soul.

SABINA: And then the firemen will come. (*She exits.*) Fire! Fire! Fire!

ALBERTO: It's Independence Day! (*He takes a running start and jumps over the flames.*) In my town I always won first prize. (*He jumps again.*) I almost burned my heels but I kept jumping. The bonfires were bigger than this terrace. A hundred times bigger! A thousand times bigger! (*He jumps again.*) Meow, meow. Where has my little kitty in heat gone?

(*He looks for her. SABINA enters making siren noises with her mouth and carrying a jug of water.*)

SABINA: The firemen! (*She pours the water and puts out the fire. She loses her balance and falls to the floor.*)

(*ALBERTO picks her up and embraces her.*)

ALBERTO: Come, let's go to the hammock.

(*With difficulty they make it to the hammock and fall into it.*)

SABINA (*In a whisper*): Who are you? Tell me who you are. You haven't told me anything about you. I don't know anything about you. My head is spinning. I'm dizzy. Give me another drink, please.

ALBERTO: No. There's no more. (*He caresses her.*)

SABINA: What's your name?

ALBERTO: Federico Garcia Lorca.

SABINA: Federico, tell me a story.

ALBERTO: Okay, and you just relax and fall asleep in my arms. Little girl, my little girl. "Hushabye, hushabye. Oh, my darling, don't you cry. Guardian angels up above, take care of the one I love."

SABINA: I'm very dizzy. Everything's going around in circles. I'm . . . Where are we?

ALBERTO: Here, on the terrace. You can see lots of things from here. A whole bunch of stars. The big dipper. The seven sisters. Venus!

SABINA: What?

ALBERTO: Shhh . . . And I can see lots of television antennas. And now, while they're all being bored by the evening news, here we are on the rooftop. . . making love. An airplane just flew over, way up high. I've never been in an airplane but it must feel a lot like this. Say . . .

(*SABINA does not answer. She is breathing deeply.*)

ALBERTO: Tomorrow I'll take the plane and I'll go to Loch Ness and do an article on the monster and sell it for big bucks. (*Tiredly.*) I'll stop selling Bibles forever. (*In a weak voice.*) They'll never say no to me . . . They'll never say no to me again. (*The doorbell rings.*) This is wild. It's like being in an airplane! (*In a whisper*). Ring . . . ring . . . ring . . . (*He falls asleep.*)

(*We hear the doorbell again. After a moment, the sound of keys in the lock and the door opening. Then some footsteps.*)

VOICE OF JEAN-LUC (*Offstage*): Sabina . . . Sabina! Je suis arrivé. Sabina! Je suis ici. Where are you?

(*JEAN-LUC appears in the doorway of the terrace. The smile freezes on his face and he remains immobile. After a moment, he leaves the keys on the table and exits. Sound of footsteps and a door closing.*)

THE END

Miriam Belichikov and Walter Raubicheck in the 1991 American premiere of *The Voucher* at Pace University in New York City. Directed by Timur Djordjadze. Production by Christopher Thomas

THE VOUCHER

CHARACTERS

Marta
Gonzalo, her husband
Never, their dog

Dining/living room of a modest furnished apartment. The furniture is typical of a rental unit: unattractive, cheap, and impersonal. The place is barely decorated. The room gives evidence of a recent move. As the lights come up, we see MARTA. She is neatly dressed and made-up although her face reveals a certain fatigue. She opens her handbag and looks for a piece of paper that she puts on the table next to the telephone. She is going to dial when she has second thoughts and hangs up. She sits on the sofa next to a box filled with clothing that she arranges carefully.

The doorbell rings. Marta gets up, starts to put on her coat, and goes to open the door. GONZALO appears in the doorway.

MARTA (*Without letting him in*): What do you want?
GONZALO: What do you mean, what do I want? I want to come in.
MARTA: Why?
GONZALO: We have to talk.
MARTA: I can't right now. I'm in a hurry. I was just going out.

(*GONZALO pushes the door and enters the room.*)

GONZALO: I think you owe me an explanation.
MARTA: Another one? I don't have any left.
GONZALO: Where is Never?
MARTA: You ought to know. She was at your place. Maybe she got tired and went out to get some fresh air.
GONZALO: She's disappeared. You're the only one who has keys to the apartment and you knew I'd be gone for two days. So you took the dog, didn't you?
MARTA (*Looking around*): Call her. She'll want to see you.
GONZALO (*Opening doors to the other rooms*): Never! (*He whistles.*) Never! Never, it's me!
MARTA: See for yourself. She's not here.

GONZALO: Where's the dog? I'm not going to get angry, Marta. I just want an explanation. You took her away from me.

MARTA: Are you going to report me to the police? I don't recommend it. You'll look totally ridiculous. (*She laughs.*) I can just see it: Outraged husband denounces wife for kidnapping affectionate little dog. (*Peals of laughter.*) That's really funny, isn't it?

GONZALO: Don't make me nervous. I'm trying to be reasonable. I ask you not to make me lose control of myself.

MARTA: Yell if you want to. It's healthy. I know you need to get it out.

GONZALO (*Raising his voice*): Stop talking to me in that tone of voice! You're going to force me into what I'm trying to avoid! Where is the dog?

MARTA: Lower your voice, please. I don't feel well at all. I haven't left the house in two days. I'm still a little . . .

GONZALO: What's wrong?

MARTA: Fever. I've had a temperature of 104.

GONZALO: Did you see a doctor?

MARTA: I've been delirious. Last night I woke up screaming. I had a terrible nightmare where you had been turned into a red spider . . .

GONZALO (*In concern*): When did you have the first symptoms? Was there pain? Inflammation? Have you been taking something for the fever? Do you want me to examine you?

MARTA: Don't worry, I'm okay now. I've been taking antibiotics and the fever's gone today. By the way, Gonzalo, when you give anesthesia to a patient during an operation, can he hear?

GONZALO: Can he hear? Well, obviously not if it's a general anesthetic.

MARTA: And if it's a light anesthetic? If it's a light general anesthetic, he can listen to what's happening around him?

GONZALO: Well, yes, but, why are you asking me this?

MARTA: No, it was just an image I had. When I was delirious with the fever I felt as if I were anesthetized. (*Short pause.*) But I could hear everything.

GONZALO: You look tired to me. You shouldn't be alone.

MARTA: When did your train get in? I expected you before. You were ten minutes late. You got into the station at 6:30, didn't you?

GONZALO: How did you know that?

MARTA: I was expecting you.

GONZALO: You knew I'd come for the dog, of course. You're admitting that you took her.

MARTA: I retrieved her. I opened the door and she came running to me. "Oh, no," I told her, and I explained her situation to her quite clearly. Then she freely decided that she preferred to live with me. I assure you that I did not coerce her.

GONZALO: You've got me puzzled now, Marta. I don't know if you're developing a new sense of humor or if you're putting me on.

MARTA (*Scornfully*): What I'm putting on is my coat. And I'm in a hurry.

GONZALO: Listen to me. We have to talk to each other like civilized people. We're screwing up each other's lives too much. There's no sense to it.

MARTA (*Showing him a poster*): What do you think about this poster over there on the wall? Everything in this place is so ugly.

GONZALO: I came here to talk to you!

MARTA: Are you going to let me have the piano? It was my father's piano. He gave it to me.

GONZALO: Shut up! I want . . . I'm fuckin' upset, Marta. Don't you see that?

MARTA (*Staring at him*): I know. You can't stand feeling abandoned. It makes you sick. Well you ought to calm down, because it's a lie. You left me first and then I . . . went away.

GONZALO: I never left you. That's not true.

MARTA: No, of course not. You just worked so much. Well, you're better now. At least you're not talking to me about diastoles and systoles.

GONZALO: I don't understand you.

MARTA: I no longer expect you to understand me. I'm a little . . . paranoid, but I'm not a blithering idiot.

GONZALO: I've always had you on my mind.

MARTA: You've always had me in the house. I have a neighbor who says the best thing about being married is that you don't have to worry any more about taking your girlfriend out.

GONZALO: Why didn't you tell me you felt this way?

MARTA: It wasn't serious. You know my fevers are psychosomatic.

GONZALO: Why didn't you tell me you were cuckolding me.

MARTA: Now there's a silly expression. Do you know where it comes from? I've never been able to figure out what it means.

GONZALO: At least if you'd managed to mess around with that schmuck discreetly, but no, you had to take him up to our apartment. So the super could see you.

MARTA: We never did it in your bed.

GONZALO: That's the least of it! I've already told you that what I can't stand is . . . I feel betrayed!

MARTA: Poor little Gonzalo, forget it, okay? It's all so boring. We don't understand each other. People can't communicate with everyone, that's normal. It's a question of vibrations. Yours and mine clash--pow!--and it's just chaos, chaos, chaos.

GONZALO: Is it over?

MARTA: I hope so. I'm trying to find peace.

GONZALO: I knew he was a son of a bitch. I'm glad that at least you've realized that.

MARTA: I was talking about chaos.

GONZALO: So you are still seeing him.
MARTA: What difference does it make?
GONZALO: You know that it makes a difference to me.
MARTA: I'm not with anybody. I already told you that I need to be alone.
GONZALO: For how long?
MARTA: Until I can forget and start to believe again in the impossible.
GONZALO: I need you to come home with me. This is absurd.
MARTA: Totally absurd. It took me a lot of effort to reach this decision, but there it is, I've made it.
GONZALO: You have to come back. I can't get used to being alone.
MARTA: You'll learn.
GONZALO: Marta, I love you. I swear to you that I love you.
MARTA: I know you do. You taught me something that I never knew.
GONZALO: Come home. We can work things out.
MARTA: You taught me the incredible aspect of love: destruction.
GONZALO: I want to go on living with you. I don't think it's too late.
MARTA: Perhaps destruction is a part of love.
GONZALO: Listen to me, Marta, I've been thinking a lot about us. I know that I've been a dumb bastard, but I'm going to make a real effort to save our relationship.
MARTA: Yes, you're a dumb bastard, and a deaf one, too.
GONZALO: You have to understand me. You know I have a lot of responsibility. I'm working so hard so they'll promote me to head the unit. I already have thirty beds under my direction. I spend ten hours a day in the operating room
MARTA: No! Not the same old damn thing again, please. I dream about people with physical deformities, attached to machines, about transfusions and EKGs. Tick-tock, tick-tock, tick-tock, hearts that never stop.
GONZALO: I'm doing it for us, for our future. I'm trying to earn money so we can live in comfort.
MARTA: That's interesting. Good luck! We made a mistake. I need something besides that, and you need a different kind of woman.
GONZALO: You're going to make me lose my patience. I've decided to forgive you, that I do understand. I know that you're a little . . . unbalanced, and I also know that I'm partly to blame. Let's help one another. If you don't give me a hand, I won't be able to get the head position.
MARTA: I don't give a shit! God, our whole life with you repeating the same damn thing.
GONZALO: You're not listening to me!
MARTA: No.
GONZALO: Is it that you're not interested in talking to me?
MARTA: Yes.
GONZALO: Yes?
MARTA: Yes, I'm not, I'm not interested.

GONZALO: Are you coming home?
MARTA: No.
GONZALO: I warn you that I'm not going to ask again.
MARTA: I'm grateful. I'm in a hurry.
GONZALO: It's your last chance.
MARTA: I don't want it.
GONZALO: I can't believe how resentful you are. You're sick.
MARTA: Yes, you give me palpitations of the heart.
GONZALO: I won't tolerate your talking to me like that!
MARTA: Go away, Gonzalo. Get out of my apartment. I didn't invite you to come here.
GONZALO: Fine, if that's what you want. But I came here for something.
MARTA: For something that's not here. (*Looking at her watch.*) Good God! It's eleven to eight! (*She crosses to the door. GONZALO steps in front of her and won't let her leave.*)
GONZALO: Stop! You're not getting out of here until you tell me where the dog is.
MARTA: Step aside. I have something urgent to do.
GONZALO: Give me back what you stole from me.
MARTA: She's mine! I raised her. I took care of her when she was sick.
GONZALO: That's nonsense. I'm the one who took her out and walked her.
MARTA: That's a lie! I fed her, I did everything for her.
GONZALO: Sure, but who paid for her?
MARTA: You don't buy something, stupid, not something alive. And step out of my way!
GONZALO: Where is the dog?
MARTA: Do you want to know where she is? You want me to tell you? She's in the municipal dog pound.
GONZALO: You put her in the pound?
MARTA: Straight from your place to the pound. What did you think? That she'd be here waiting for you?
GONZALO: Why you bitch!
MARTA: And don't bother going to get her because they aren't going to give her to you. I have the paper that says I'm the owner and they'll only hand her over if you give them the voucher.
GONZALO: Give me that paper this minute!
MARTA: You've taken everything from me, but you're never going to see the dog again! (*MARTA again attempts to leave. GONZALO grabs her.*) Let me out! I have to leave!
GONZALO: The paper!
MARTA: This evening's the deadline for claiming her. The pound closes at eight. I only have eight minutes left. (*Hysterical.*) Eight minutes!

GONZALO: Why?
MARTA: They gave me seventy-two hours. If I don't go right now and they close, they'll put her to sleep.
GONZALO: That's a lie!
MARTA: I swear to God. (*Crying.*) I've been sick and alone. I wasn't able to go outside before. When you came, I was just going to get her. Please, I beg you, let me go. I don't have any more time!
GONZALO: No.

(*MARTA throws herself at him and begins hitting him.*)

MARTA: You son of a bitch! You're a . . . They going to kill her and it's your fault!
GONZALO: It's yours. You're the one who took her to the slaughterhouse.
MARTA (*Pleading*): I still have time. The pound's practically next door. There are still four minutes.
GONZALO: No.
MARTA (*Handing him the voucher*): Here, you go. Run, I'll tell you where it is.
GONZALO: No.
MARTA: What? You're not going to get her?
GONZALO: You have to pay for your crazy whims. (*He reads the paper and looks at his watch.*) That's it. Time's up.
MARTA: It's you. I can see it so well, so clearly. I feel a kind of happiness at knowing I wasn't mistaken. You're despicable. You are the red spider; you've eaten my roots, my leaves . . . you've killed my dog . . .
GONZALO: You killed her. You're crazy, Marta. Out of pride . . .
MARTA: Out of hatred.
GONZALO: You're worse off than I thought.
MARTA: You can feel satisfied with your work, doctor.
GONZALO: Eight o'clock.
MARTA: Goodbye.
GONZALO: Wait a minute. I have to make sure. (*He goes over to the telephone.*)
MARTA: What are you going to do?
GONZALO: Call the pound. (*GONZALO dials the number, waits, and then hangs up*. They're closed. (*With satisfaction.*) Your doggy's already . . . (*He makes the motions of giving an injection and tears the paper into pieces. MARTA collapses.*) Goodbye. (*He exits.*)

(*MARTA looks at the door, waits several seconds, and suddenly begins to laugh loudly. She runs over to one of the packing boxes and opens it. NEVER comes out, stretching.*)

MARTA (*Surprised*): You're already awake? Poor little thing. That's good, you behaved marvelously. (*She gives the dog something to eat.*) Did you hear, Never? I needed for you to hear all of it, so you'd know what your father's like. Well, now you're going to feel more lively. It was just a little dream. (*She takes a syringe out of the box.*) It was Gonzalo's fault; this was his. (*She tosses it down scornfully.*) You see how everything turned out okay? I know him so well. You know, even I thought it was true; I almost died. But it's over, and he'll never bother us again. . .or at least, not you. Shall we go out for a walk? Come on. . .

(*NEVER wags her tail happily. MARTA picks up the leash. They exit.*)

THE END

The Teatro Imaginario acting company of Zaragoza, on the set of *Noches de amor efímero (Nights of Passing Love)*, 1996. Directed by Alfonso Desentre.

A NIGHT IN THE SUBWAY

CHARACTERS

Carmen, a government employee
José, an unemployed laborer

The deserted platform of a subway station. CARMEN enters. She is in her late thirties and is dressed in an elegant but conventional style. Her hair has been done at a beauty salon and she has long, polished finger nails. With a certain uneasiness, she sits down on a bench to wait. After a few moments, JOSE enters. He is a young, muscular man with dark skin. CARMEN is startled when she sees him, but covers up her reaction. The young man sits down on another bench and lights a cigarette. He looks at Carmen. CARMEN nervously walks up and down the platform. After a moment, JOSE starts to approach her. CARMEN, frightened, clutches her purse and crosses to the exit.

JOSE *(Calling out to her)*: Hey you . . . *(He catches up to her.)*

CARMEN *(Very frightened and speaking quickly)*: I don't have anything. came into the subway because I've no money left. Not a dime, I swear to you. Here. *(She hands him the purse.)* You can have it. My watch is a good one. Here, you can sell it. My rings. . . I can't get them off! Please, not the fingers. Don't cut off my fingers.

JOSE *(Interrupting her in bewilderment)*: What are you saying? What's wrong with you? Did I ask you for something?

CARMEN: What do you want? What do you want from me?

JOSE: Goddamn. You're scared out of your mind, ain't that so? I really look that bad, huh?

CARMEN: No, no, it's just that . . . it's very late. I'm not used to being out alone at this time of the night. I never take the subway and . . .

JOSE: Yeah, by this time you're home glued to the TV. *(CARMEN nods.)* Here, take your things and relax. Just be calm.

CARMEN *(Returning to the bench and sitting down)*: What did you want?

JOSE: I was going to ask if you'd been waiting a long time.

CARMEN: Yes, quite a while. They told me that the last train hadn't come yet.

JOSE: There's always a big wait with the last one. *(He looks at his watch.)* Though it should of been here by now.

CARMEN *(Looking toward the tunnel)*: I think it's coming.

JOSE *(Pause)*: I don't hear it.

CARMEN: No, I don't either.
JOSE: Well, we'll just have to wait. *(He takes a package of sandwiches out of his backpack.)* Care for one?
CARMEN *(Without looking at him)*: No thanks. I don't smoke.

(CARMEN paces nervously along the platform.)

JOSE: Stand still, lady, you're making me dizzy. Are you hungry?
CARMEN: No thank you.
JOSE: They're ham. *(CARMEN continues pacing without paying attention to him.)* Say, they're ham.
CARMEN: So what?
JOSE: They're ham sandwiches. Don't you want some?
CARMEN: No, really, thanks anyway. I just had supper.

(CARMEN continues pacing, more and more nervously.)

JOSE: In a restaurant?
CARMEN: What?
JOSE: Did you have supper in a restaurant?
CARMEN: Yes.
JOSE: Alone?
CARMEN: It's taking too long.
JOSE: Huh?
CARMEN: The subway. It's not normal for a subway train to take so long.
JOSE: The last one does. Sometimes it takes forever. Why don't you sit down?
CARMEN: No, thank you. I prefer to stand.
JOSE: That's up to you.
CARMEN: Thank you.
JOSE: Why?
CARMEN: Why what?
JOSE: So why are you always thanking me? I don't get it.
CARMEN: Oh, I don't know. *(Walking away.)* Good Lord, it's taking so long!
JOSE *(Raising his voice)*: Did you have supper alone in the restaurant?
CARMEN: No.
JOSE: With your boyfriend?
CARMEN: Good Lord! The train's never going to come!
JOSE: Well, there's not a soul in sight. Maybe it's broken down and stuck in the tunnel.
CARMEN: I hope not.
JOSE: You have to get up early tomorrow?

CARMEN *(Facing him, frightened)*: Why did you say that?
JOSE: Say what?
CARMEN: Why did you ask if I have to get up early tomorrow?
JOSE: Goddamn, you'd think I asked your bra size!
CARMEN: Well, I'm leaving.
JOSE: Don't be such a prude. I was just joking. I asked in case you work. You gotta job?
CARMEN: Yes. Why?
JOSE: When I'm workin' I hit the sack early so I can pull my weight. But now I've been laid off. Look. *(He takes off his jacket and unbuttons his shirt. CARMEN screams.)* What's wrong?
CARMEN: What are you doing?
JOSE: I'm going to show you my scar. See, a girder came loose and fell on me. It almost wiped out my tatoo. *(CARMEN doesn't know where to go. JOSE calmly keeps on talking.)* I had a build like a movie star, and now it's messed up. They don't let poor bastards like me be beautiful, you know. That's something I've always thought, how beautiful people are who've got plenty of dough. It's not the fancy clothes or the shining hair or the jewels. No, it's the skin. It's the fuckin' skin that makes you different. Say, by the way, you have really silky skin. What are you doing in this sewer at this time of night?
CARMEN: I'm leaving. The train isn't coming. I'll try to get a cab.
JOSE: Didn't you say you were out of dough?
CARMEN: I don't have any here. I'll pay when I get home. That's what I should have done in the first place. Yes, I'm leaving. Goodbye.
JOSE: Okay, lady, goodbye.

(CARMEN quickly exits. JOSE finishes his sandwich. He takes out a small liquor bottle and takes a swig. From time to time, he looks toward the tunnel. To pass the time, he starts to hum or sing. CARMEN enters, hysterical.)

CARMEN: It's locked! The doors to the street are locked!
JOSE: What the fuck!
CARMEN: And there's nobody there! Nobody! No token clerks, no guards, not a single employee. There's nobody!
JOSE: Calm down. Come on, lady, calm down. The last train has to come.
CARMEN *(Terrified)*: And what if there is no last train? What if the last one has already gone by?
JOSE: Then they wouldn't have let us in.
CARMEN: And what if they made a mistake? What if letting us in was a mistake and no other train comes?

JOSE *(After a pause)*: Well, anyway we won't be cold here. We won't be sleeping without a roof over our heads.

CARMEN: Don't even joke about it. Good Lord, it can't be! This is a nightmare! Please, go see if you can find someone. Let's both go.

JOSE: And if the train comes while we're gone, then what?

CARMEN: You go. I'll wait.

JOSE: Yeah. And if it comes, I'm stuck here alone.

CARMEN: I'll tell them to wait for you. Please! Please, I beg you!

JOSE: Hey, hey. Come on. Calm down. They can't have left us locked up in here. We'll wait a few more minutes. If the train doesn't come, I'll go look for someone.

CARMEN *(Half crying)*: There's nobody. I saw that there was nobody. *(Yelling.)* Hello! Hello! Is anybody there? Anybody at all?

JOSE: Relax, lady. If anybody's there, you'll scare them away.

CARMEN: The train's not coming! Don't you see? There aren't any more trains.

JOSE: All right, all right, I'll go see what's up.

CARMEN: I'm going with you.

JOSE *(Taking hold of her hand as a natural gesture)*: Let's go.

CARMEN *(Pulling away in fear and disgust)*: I'm staying here.

JOSE: Okay, it's better for you to wait just in case. *(He starts to leave and CARMEN follows him.)* What are you doing?

CARMEN: It's . . . better for me to go with you.

JOSE: It's better for you to wait in case it comes. Maybe it broke down in the tunnel and . . . that's why it's late.

CARMEN *(Doubtful)*: Well, but don't be long, please.

JOSE *(Taking a swig and passing her the bottle)*: Here, have a swig, that'll calm your nerves. I'll be right back.

(JOSE exits. CARMEN remains alone. She looks at the bottle but can't decide to have a drink. Then she takes a handkerchief out of her purse, wipes off the bottle carefully, and drinks.)

CARMEN *(Calling out toward the tunnel)*: Is anybody there? Please! Can anybody hear me? I'm down here! I'm down here!

(JOSE enters.)

JOSE: There's not a soul there.

CARMEN *(Crying)*: I have to get home. I want to be home.

JOSE: Don't cry. Here, have another drink.

CARMEN: No, I don't drink. A telephone? Isn't there a phone here?

JOSE *(Shaking his head)*: All I've seen is a machine with chocolate bars. Here, I got two.

CARMEN: The chocolate's stale.

JOSE *(With growing self-assurance)*: If we're going to spend the night here, we need the calories.

CARMEN: It just can't be. They can't leave us locked up all night. It's impossible.

JOSE: Stranger things than that have happened to me. *(He tosses her a candy bar.)*

CARMEN *(Trying to calm herself)*: What are we going to do?

JOSE: For now, we'll have a cigarette.

CARMEN: No, I don't smoke. I want to get out of here.

JOSE: Wait, let me think. *(He thinks.)* The only thing I can think of is to take the tunnel and try to reach the next station. It's a busier stop than this one . . .

CARMEN: Are you crazy?

JOSE: It's the only solution.

CARMEN: No, the tunnels are filled with rats that big. At night they come out. We'd run into them. They'd bite our legs . . .

JOSE: Hey, stop it already! When people go by, rats get out of the way.

CARMEN *(Pointing toward the tunnel)*: That's their territory. Don't you see?

JOSE: There's no other way. We either take a walk or we sleep here.

CARMEN: Let's go!

JOSE: Okay.

(They approach the track. CARMEN looks down, terrified.)

CARMEN: I can't jump. It's too high.

JOSE: I'll jump first and lift you down.

CARMEN: I weigh too much.

JOSE *(Showing off his strength, he lifts her in his arms)*: I could even jump carrying you.

CARMEN *(Kicking her legs)*: No, no. Let go of me.

JOSE: What gives with you? Do you want to get out of here or not?

CARMEN: Yes.

JOSE: Well, come on.

CARMEN: And my heels? I can't walk down there with these high heels.

JOSE: Take them off.

CARMEN: Barefoot? How horrible! They'd bite my feet . . .

JOSE: Say, what's wrong with you?

CARMEN *(After a pause)*: It scares me. I'm panicked.

JOSE: All right. I'll go alone. It doesn't scare me. I'm used to sewers and crap. You wait here. I'll come back to get you.

(JOSE he is about to jump, CARMEN stops him.)

CARMEN: Hey.
JOSE: What do you want?
CARMEN: What's your name?
JOSE: José. What's yours?
CARMEN: Carmen.
JOSE: See you in a few minutes, Carmen.
CARMEN *(Grabbing him)*: José, what if you get to the other station and it's closed too?
JOSE: The next station is bigger. It has an office, I think.
CARMEN: What if there's nobody there either?
JOSE: We've got nothing to lose.
CARMEN: Yes we do. We'll be separated, with each of us in a different station.
JOSE *(Pause)*: Listen, Carmen, if nobody's there, I'll come back to be with you.
CARMEN: You're very . . . nice. Thank you.
JOSE *(Giving her an affectionate pat on the face)*: It'll be a pleasure. Goddamn!
CARMEN: What's wrong?
JOSE: I'm a genius! A blooming genius! Carrying everything you own around with ya has its advantages. I've got a flashlight in the old backpack!
CARMEN: Oh good! That way you'll get there faster.

(JOSE opens the backpack and takes out the flashlight.)

JOSE: Here, you keep the bottle and the cigarettes. If you get nervous, have a smoke.
CARMEN: But I've never smoked a cigarette.
JOSE: You've never been locked up in a subway station neither, have you? You stay here, sit down and relax. If you get nervous, have a swig and a few drags. And if somebody shows up, you'll rescue me, agreed? *(He gets ready to jump.)*
CARMEN: José! *(JOSE looks at her.)* What if people show up in the two stations and they let us out at different doors?
JOSE: What?
CARMEN: Never mind. It was just a silly thought . . .
JOSE: What silly thought?
CARMEN *(Blushing)*: That . . . that I'd still have your bottle and your cigarettes.
JOSE *(Smiling)*: So enjoy. *(He's about to jump but turns around.)* I don't have a phone. Will you give me your number just in case?
CARMEN: Of course.

(CARMEN takes a business card out of her purse.)

JOSE *(Reading it)*: What the fuck! Such an important woman! Chief of the Bureau of Bibliographic Information of the Ministry of Culture. What's that?

CARMEN: An office filled with papers and white collars.

JOSE: Whatever, ma'am, I'm going.

CARMEN: Don't be long. *(Just as JOSE jumps, the lights on the platform go out.)* They've turned out the light! Hello! Is anybody there? Help! Help! We're down here! We're down here!

JOSE *(After climbing back up)*: Save your breath. These lights are automatic. Come here. Sit down on the bench and wait for me. I have to get there in a hurry.

CARMEN: José, don't go. Don't leave me alone.

JOSE: But . . .

CARMEN: Give me your hand, please. I'm afraid. Stay here with me.

JOSE: But nobody's going to come down here until morning.

CARMEN: No, don't let go, please.

JOSE: Hey, stop trembling like that. Come on. Nothing's going to happen. I'm here with you. Here, have a cigarette. *(JOSE sits down beside her and lights a cigarette. He lights another for himself. CARMEN smokes. JOSE shines his flashlight on her.)* The smoke takes your mind off it, right?

CARMEN: I don't know. I just don't know anymore.

JOSE: Well, stop trembling, baby. *(He gives her a hug.)* Nothing's going to happen to you. Can't you see that I'm here?

CARMEN: You're . . . you're very brave.

JOSE: Worse things than this have happened to me. And I do mean worse. Why this is like being locked up in a castle with a princess.

CARMEN: What will my husband think when I don't show up tonight?

JOSE: You've got a husband, too? Shit, you've got it all!

CARMEN: He's going to think that I'm off somewhere with a lover.

JOSE: You got lovers besides?

CARMEN: No! Never! I've never had a lover. *(Pause.)* I've never failed to go home to sleep. Do you have a girlfriend?

JOSE: Not hardly! Nobody loves a guy out of work. I had a girl, a real doll, a brunette like you, but when they tossed me out on the street, she took up with some dumbass who's got a future.

CARMEN: A future?

JOSE: Yeah. He's getting a professional degree.

CARMEN: Some future.

JOSE: That's what I say. I know the future's not in stinkin' money. Even if everybody else says so, I know that the future's not in money.

CARMEN: Do you know where it is?

JOSE: Look, baby, I know it sounds funny . . . I think that the future . . . is in love, in people caring about each other.

CARMEN *(Speaking quickly)*: I couldn't agree with you more, José. Money makes men cowardly, obsessed, boring, fat, fat . . . fat. Oh, good Lord, I don't know what I'm saying anymore!

JOSE *(Laughing)*: Is your husband fat?

CARMEN: Shh. Be quiet. It's . . . it's just that you make me nervous.

JOSE: Me?

CARMEN: You're so close. No, don't you dare move away.

JOSE *(Drawing closer)*: The thought would never cross my mind, princess.

CARMEN: May I see your tattoo?

JOSE: Sure.

(He unbuttons his shirt. CARMEN shines the flashlight on him.)

CARMEN: What a pretty butterfly.

JOSE: Well, if you touch it, it moves its wings.

CARMEN *(Touching it)*: How pretty, it looks real, with its little antennae and all . . . and its little feelers . . . and its little eyes . . . and its . . . Hug me!

JOSE *(Hugging her)*: Are you still cold?

CARMEN: What a strong chest you have. What strong arms. Oh my God . . .

JOSE *(Embracing her tightly):* And it's all for you.

CARMEN: Turn off the flashlight.

JOSE: Not afraid anymore?

CARMEN: Afraid? With this protective wall? Turn off the flashlight.

JOSE: What if the train comes?

CARMEN: Let it go by. Let it go by.

(JOSE turns off the flashlight. In the darkness we hear kissing and whispering.)

THE END

DIRECTING PALOMA PEDRERO

My love affair with the Spanish theatre began many years ago. It was the early fifties: A beautiful country seemingly at the end of the world--Georgia. An exquisite nineteenth-century theatre with gilt-framed mirrors, dark burgundy velvet seats, and dusty crystal chandeliers. In the midst of the crowd, wildly applauding at the finale of *Fuente Ovejuna* stands a little boy who cannot appreciate the depth of Lope de Vega's masterpiece, but, like everyone else in the audience is emotionally involved in the gripping drama. This little boy is me. Does it sound very Fellini-esque? Yes, it was.

Much later, when my studies, teaching, and directing brought me to Moscow, Washington, Chicago, Boston, and finally to New York, my love affair with the Spanish theatre--with Lope de Vega, Cervantes, Calderón, Tirso de Molina, García Lorca--continued. And finally in 1991 I worked on three one-act plays by the contemporary Spanish playwright, Paloma Pedrero: *The Color of August, A Night Divided,* and *The Voucher.* What an experience it was!

There is a reason for my naming this group of brilliant Spanish playwrights, for Paloma Pedrero in many ways carries on the best traditions of the Spanish theatre. In this essay I will touch upon only some of them.

First of all, the action. It was such a refreshing experience to work on a contemporary playwright who understands theatre as a visual art. There was no need to struggle, as happens so often, to build artificially a physical action that does not exist in the play. In Pedrero's plays the conflicts, relationships, even characters, are presented through justifiable physical action, the trademark of the Spanish theatre since its Golden Age. She is extremely creative in constructing fast-moving, energetic plots, which not only explain or illustrate the texts, but also create logical--or, in some cases, illogical--undercurrents to events or relationships. One example I cannot resist giving is from *The Color of August.* At the peak of the conflict between Maria and Laura, the playwright suggests the insertion of an improvised wedding scene, which in an ingenious physical way brings out more clearly the bizarre thoughts and hidden desires that were already hinted at in the text. And everything falls into place.

The second important quality is the extremely complex and intriguing female characters. For me it was obvious from the beginning that Ms. Pedrero's main object of study, revelation, and dissection is woman. In some cases I had the feeling that she brought herself into the plays and subsequently onto the stage, where without pseudo-shame or embarrassment she revealed her own personal and intimate conflicts, troubles, and questions, and did so with tremendous honesty and dignity. During meetings with the cast, there were a lot of discussions: are these plays feminist, are some of the characters lesbians or bi-sexual or man haters? It was my understanding from my first reading, reinforced by discussions with the translator and talks with cast members, that the plays are about contemporary women, about their lives, frustrations, loves, passion, and deceptions, which, like everything in today's reality, take different forms. It is important to note in this regard that women and men are treated equally. There is no blame placed on men, nor are women's problems justified by their "weakness," "tenderness," or other such clichés. To my great delight, after talking with Ms. Pedrero I found that I had no reason to change this interpretation. I was right. Her characters are simply women.

A few more words about the roles men and women play in Pedrero's works. In the course of the plays, men are noticeably absent; even when they appear on stage, they arrive at the very end to mumble deliberately meaningless text. Sometimes, to make matters even worse, Pedrero has them speak in a foreign language. Men are revealed as petty, egocentric, extremely naive, and at the same time vicious and pitiless creatures. In most cases the women are much stronger, more calculating, although often disturbed; they manage to manipulate, deceive, and play with the men, unfortunately gaining very little. Women are the ones who initiate conflict, are in charge during the whole fight, and lose. One more rare quality of the plays in this context is that the female characters use men's love and sexuality as a weapon to win each other and achieve erotic satisfaction. Contrary to traditional relationships in which two women fight for the man, here the male character is used to gain, or regain, another woman's love, friendship, and companionship.

The third quality I would like to mention is the language. First of all, Pedrero manages to bring into her plays the forgotten art of verbal action. The texts themselves have action contained in them. They are far from the so-called "soap opera" and "sit-com" aesthetics we are so used to lately. Her texts have a very intriguing, chameleon-like quality. During readings and rehearsal, I found that it was impossible to reach a once-and-for-all fixed interpretation of the characters, events, and of the entire play. Parts of the text which we would at first interpret as funny, light, and charming suddenly would develop darker sado-masochistic meaning, and vice versa. Very strangely, I got the feeling that the texts of Pedrero's plays acquired a life of their own, and in some cases would lead you in their own direction, even when you might disagree with them. I would like to mention one more thing about the verbal texture of the plays: what some might call their indecent or obscene language. It is true that Ms. Pedrero sometimes describes sexual acts and body parts in graphic terms that a segment of the American audience--in contrast to the Europeans--might find risqué, even offensive. But one must note that the language is never tasteless or vulgar, is always justifiable in terms of character development and relationships.

If space permitted, there are many more things I could write about the rewarding experience of directing Ms. Pedrero's plays. It was exciting, educational, and rewarding for me and for everyone involved in the production. I would only like to add that it is my great wish that the three plays I directed, and others written by Ms. Pedrero, will find their way to a wider American audience and deserved success and recognition. I think that all of us in the United States can learn a lot from them about today's society and the difficult, important, and sometimes cruel part that women play in it.

Timur Djordjadze
Associate Professor
Theatre & Fine Arts Department
Pace University

CRITICAL REACTION TO THE PLAYS

"*The Color of August* is the ardor of conflict in the summer of life, in the storm of emotional and social confusion. Theatre that is theatrical, young and daring."

Lorenzo López Sancho
ABC (Madrid), June 1993

"In *Nights of Passing Love* . . . we again find the themes that interest Paloma Pedrero: the intersection of loneliness and love in urban life; the chance meetings, along with the problems of passion, freedom, and independence of people who seem close to us. The author remains faithful to the formula she expressed in 1988 with *The Color of August*: a warm, lively theatre that touches young audiences."

José Henríquez
La Guía del Ocio (Madrid), 1993

"Stories of a night of love without any apparent future . . . . The spectators, sensitive to the humor, are delighted . . . . The audience's response could not be warmer."

Raymonde Temkine
Révolution (Paris), June 1994

"The staging of *A Night Divided* was the highlight of the production at The Pace Downtown Theatre . . . . After a series of comical misunderstandings that stress the characters' incapacity to communicate, the bubbles of the champagne help them to discover a way out of their emotionally barren lives into one filled with companionship, affection and physical attraction."

William García
Gestos (Irvine, CA), April 1993

"[*The Voucher*] highlights not only fiction-within-the-fiction but also other typical themes of Pedrero's theatre: loneliness, frustration, psychological instability of character, and a bitter and ironic conclusion."

Patricia W. O'Connor
Dramaturgas españolas de hoy, Madrid, 1988

TRANSLATOR'S NOTES AND ACKNOWLEDGEMENTS

Three of these translations were undertaken at the instigation of Professor Iride Lamartina-Lens, of the Modern Language Department at Pace University, who had interested theatre professor Timur Djordjadze in directing the works of Paloma Pedrero. I am indebted to the director and actors of the 1991 Pace production for their insights in reaching our goal: a stageable text. That production was supported in part by the Consulate General of Spain in New York. The translations were prepared with assistance from the Dirección General del Libro y Biblioteca of the Spanish Ministry of Culture, and the original edition was published with support from The Program of Cultural Cooperation Between Spain's Ministry of Culture and United States's Universities.

Following a long battle, Timur Djordjadze died of cancer in 1994. The first edition of *Parting Gestures* was a tribute to his encouragement, enthusiasm and creativity. This revised edition is dedicated to his memory.

Paloma Pedrero's plays have contemporary settings and characters; they therefore present few problems of cultural gaps and require minimal modifications. In the process of preparing the translations for staging, I was fortunate in having the full cooperation of the author. The few necessary changes were made with her approval. These changes appear primarily in *A Night Divided*. They include names that might pose difficulties in pronunciation or have inappropriate connotations: for example, Adolfo became Alberto, and the stage name Luna Aláez was changed to Venus Vega. In the same play, Doc Pomus and Mort Shuman's "Hushabye" was substituted for a Spanish lullaby and Independence Day for *la noche de San Juan* (midsummer night's eve), a celebration unfamiliar to American audiences. *A Night in the Subway*, which was previously titled *Tonight We're Alone*, has been renamed at the suggestion of the author.

The original edition of *Parting Gestures* would not have been possible without Martha T. Halsey, founding editor of ESTRENO Contemporary Spanish Plays. I should like to express my appreciation to her, for her tireless efforts and continuing guidance; to Marion P. Holt, for his always helpful advice on theatrical translation; to Felicia Hardison Londré, for her careful reading of the plays; to Peter Podol for his suggestions on *The Voucher*; and to Helen June, for her recommendations on American music.

I am indebted as well to young directors, like Christopher Mack and Eric Ruffin, who have recently lent their talents to performances of Pedrero's plays as we continue in our efforts to bring her voice to the American stage, and to colleagues in the United States and the United Kingdom who have called these translations to the attention of their students and local theatre groups.

My thanks also to Ellen Bay, Margrette Brown and Leonardo Mazzara for their help in preparing the camera-ready copy for this revised, expanded edition.

P. Z.

ABOUT THE TRANSLATOR

Phyllis Zatlin is Professor of Spanish and coordinator of translator training in the Department of Spanish and Portuguese of Rutgers, The State University of New Jersey. A specialist in contemporary theatre, she has published numerous books, editions, and articles on the subject. Among her published play translations from Spanish and French are Jaime Salom's *Bonfire at Dawn*, José Luis Alonso de Santos' *Going Down to Marrakesh* and *Hostages in the Barrio*, Eduardo Manet's *Lady Strass*, and Jean-Paul Daumas's *The Elephant Graveyard*. Several of her theatrical translations have been staged or presented in staged readings. *Going Down to Marrakesh* received its American premiere at the University of Missouri-Kansas City, in 1992, under the direction of Francis Cullinan. *Lady Strass* was produced professionally in New York City in 1996 at Ubu Repertory Theater, under the direction of André Ernotte. The translations of works by Paloma Pedrero, included in the present volume, have been performed at various locations in the United States and England.

ESTRENO: CONTEMPORARY SPANISH PLAYS SERIES

General Editor: Phyllis Zatlin

No. 1 Jaime Salom: ***Bonfire at Dawn*** *(Una hoguera al amanecer)*
Translated by Phyllis Zatlin. 1992.
ISBN: 0-9631212-0-0

No. 2 José López Rubio: ***In August We Play the Pyrenees*** *(Celos del aire)*
Translated by Marion Peter Holt. 1992.
ISBN: 0-9631212-1-9

No. 3 Ramón del Valle-Inclán: ***Savage Acts: Four Plays*** (*Ligazón, La rosa de papel, La cabeza del Bautista, Sacrilegio*)
Translated by Robert Lima. 1993.
ISBN: 0-9631212-2-7

No. 4 Antonio Gala: ***The Bells of Orleans*** *(Los buenos días perdidos)*
Translated by Edward Borsoi. 1993.
ISBN: 0-9631212-3-5

No. 5 Antonio Buero-Vallejo: ***The Music Window*** *(Música cercana)*
Translated by Marion Peter Holt. 1994.
ISBN: 0-9631212-4-3

No. 6 Paloma Pedrero: ***Parting Gestures with A Night in the Subway*** *(El color de agosto, La noche dividida, Resguardo personal, Solos esta noche)*
Translated by Phyllis Zatlin. Revised edition. 1999.
ISBN: 1-888463-06-6

** If you have previously ordered an original 1994 edition Volume No.6, you may purchase the revised 1999 edition for $5.00.

No. 7 Ana Diosdado: ***Yours for the Asking***
(Usted también podrá disfrutar de ella)
Translated by Patricia W. O'Connor. 1995.
ISBN: 0-9631212-6-X

No. 8 Manuel Martínez Mediero: ***A Love Too Beautiful***
(Juana del amor hermoso)
Translated by Hazel Cazorla. 1995.
ISBN: 0-9631212-7-8

No. 9 Alfonso Vallejo: ***Train to Kiu*** *(El cero transparente)*
Translated by H. Rick Hite. 1996.
ISBN: 0-9631212-8-6

No. 10 Alfonso Sastre: ***The Abandoned Doll. Young Billy Tell.*** (*Historia de una muñeca abandonada. El único hijo de William Tell*)
Translated by Carys Evans-Corrales. 1996.
ISBN: 1-888463-00-7

No. 11 Lauro Olmo and Pilar Encisco: ***The Lion Calls a Meeting. The Lion Foiled. The Lion in Love.*** (*Asamblea general. Los leones*)
Translated by Carys Evans-Corrales. 1997.
ISBN: 1-888463-01-5

No. 12 José Luis Alonso de Santos: ***Hostages in the Barrio.*** (*La estanquera de Vallecas*)
Translated by Phyllis Zatlin. 1997.
ISBN: 1-888463-02-3

No. 13 Fermín Cabal: ***Passage***. (*Travesía*)
Translated by H. Rick Hite. 1998.
ISBN: 1-888463-03-1

No. 14 Antonio Buero-Vallejo: ***The Sleep of Reason*** (*El sueño de la razón*)
Translated by Marion Peter Holt. 1998.
ISBN: 1-888463-04-X

No. 15 Fernando Arrabal: ***The Body-Builder's Book of Love*** *(Breviario de amor de un halterófilo)*
Translated by Lorenzo Mans. 1999.
ISBN: 1-888463-05-8

No. 16 Luis Araújo: ***Vanzetti***. *(Vanzetti)*
Translated by Mary Alice Lessing. 1999.
ISBN: 1-888463-08-2

ORDER FORM

List price, nos. 1-11: $6; revised ed. no. 6 and nos. 12-16, $8.
Shipping and handling for one or two volumes, $1.25 each.
Free postage on orders of three or more volumes.
Special price for complete set of 16 volumes, $85

Please indicate below quantities and titles of plays: TOTAL

___ ____ ________
___ ____ ________
___ ____ ________
___ ____ ________
___ ____ ________
___ ____ ________

Shipping & handling ________
AMOUNT ENCLOSED ________

Name and address: ____

____

____

Make checks payable to ESTRENO Plays and send to:

ESTRENO Plays
Dept. of Spanish & Portuguese, FAS
Rutgers, The State University of New Jersey
105 George St.
New Brunswick, NJ 08901-1414

For information on discounts available to bookstores, contact:
FAX: 1-732/ 932-9837 Phone: 1-732/932-9412x25
E-mail: ESTRPLAY@rci.rutgers.edu

For updated information, please visit our website:

www.rci.rutgers.edu/~estrplay/webpage.html